CONTENTS

New Directions for
Child and Adolescent
Development

Reed W. Larson
Lene Arnett Jensen
EDITORS-IN-CHIEF

William Damon
FOUNDING EDITOR

The Modernization of Youth Transitions in Europe

Manuela du Bois-Reymond
Lynne Chisholm
EDITORS

Number 113 • Fall 2006
Jossey-Bass
San Francisco

THE MODERNIZATION OF YOUTH TRANSITIONS IN EUROPE
Manuela du Bois-Reymond, Lynne Chisholm (eds.)
New Directions for Child and Adolescent Development, no. 113
Reed W. Larson, Lene Arnett Jensen, Editors-in-Chief

Microfilm copies of issues and articles are available in 16mm and 35mm, as well as microfiche in 105mm, through University Microfilms, Inc., 300 North Zeeb Road, Ann Arbor, Michigan 48106-1346.

ISSN 1520-3247   electronic ISSN 1534-8687

NEW DIRECTIONS FOR CHILD AND ADOLESCENT DEVELOPMENT is part of The Jossey-Bass Education Series and is published quarterly by Wiley Subscription Services, Inc., a Wiley company, at Jossey-Bass, 989 Market Street, San Francisco, California 94103-1741. Periodicals postage paid at San Francisco, California, and at additional mailing offices. Postmaster: Send address changes to New Directions for Child and Adolescent Development, Jossey-Bass, 989 Market Street, San Francisco, CA 94103-1741.

New Directions for Child and Adolescent Development is indexed in PsycInfo, Biosciences Information Service, Current Index to Journals in Education (ERIC), Psychological Abstracts, and Sociological Abstracts.

SUBSCRIPTIONS cost $90.00 for individuals and $240.00 for institutions, agencies, and libraries.

EDITORIAL CORRESPONDENCE should be e-mailed to the editors-in-chief: Reed W. Larson (larsonr@uiuc.edu) and Lene Arnett Jensen (jensenl@cua.edu).

Jossey-Bass Web address: www.josseybass.com

1

Europe is a rapidly changing world region in all respects, and this has consequences for young people, too. In this opening introductory chapter, the editors outline key distinctive parameters of contemporary modernization in Europe as a whole and indicate the ways in which the following chapters each contribute to a richer apprecia-tion of how modernization is affecting youth transitions.

Young Europeans in a Changing World

Manuela du Bois-Reymond, Lynne Chisholm

The authors in this volume report what it is like to be young in the rapidly changing, enormously diverse world region that is early 21st-century Europe. The chapters privilege a decidedly sociological analysis of youth as a social and cultural construction and sets of contemporary social and cultural practices characteristic of young people and young adults living in European societies. In doing so, they signal a dual conviction. First, con-ceptualizing and understanding child and adolescent development also require the more structural perspectives that sociologists bring to macrolevel and microlevel theorizing. Second, the authors in this volume use the terms *youth* and *young people* rather than *adolescence* and *adoles-cents*, and they routinely introduce the terms *young adulthood* and *young adults* into their analyses. In this way, they underline the importance of research perspectives anchored in the study of the life course as a histori-cally and culturally specific social phenomenon. Furthermore, this phe-nomenon is firmly situated within the large-scale economic and political change processes currently taking place in Europe and in the global con-text of Europe as a world region in interaction with other world regions.

As a North American–based series with a largely North American read-ership, the New Directions series has published content that has naturally centered on North American debates and research findings. This issue

We would like to express our sincere thanks to Lene Arnett Jensen and Reed Larson, who encouraged us to bring this collection to fruition with unswerving enthusiasm and trust in its value.

presents ideas and information from Europe, with the aim of complementing North American debates and strengthening communication between youth research scholars across the disciplines and across the Atlantic. In the past fifteen years or so, interdisciplinary European youth research has emerged and expanded so that there is both greater permeability between national-linguistic academic discourses and more intercultural, comparative research. Today's European youth research community is lively and dynamic, but it is not well known in North American scholarly circles, with the partial exception of youth (sub)cultural studies or the critical analysis of schooling and social and cultural reproduction. This volume should prompt, then, the professional curiosity of North American specialists in youth studies, particularly those working at the interface of research, policy, and practice.

Language, Culture, and Research Discourse

English has become the global scientific lingua franca. This has set the direction for Europe, where English increasingly dominates scientific discourse. This means that linguistic flexibility has effectively become a core professional competence for European youth research specialists who work interculturally and comparatively. At the least, they must be able to read the research literature in two and preferably three languages. This is simply not the case for most North American scholars, whatever their discipline, and they are much less likely to be aware of important and interesting ideas and information coming from Europe. These ideas could stimulate and enrich North American discourse, just as the Europeans' facility with English self-evidently contribute to European discourse through the combined Anglo-American literature.

However, language is by no means simply a technical communication tool: it carries and expresses cultural meanings to which multiple language skills by definition open access, at least in principle. Grasping and working with cultural meanings are definitive features of the construction of knowledge in the humanities and social sciences (and, many would now argue, in the natural and applied sciences). Cultural and linguistic diversity is Europe's hallmark; in many ways, this defines Europeans' understandings of the world region in which they live.

From within their own locations and in communication with each other, Europeans hence approach the "youth question" in distinctive ways among themselves and in comparison with North Americans. This does not mean that European and North American societies and discourses share little; quite the reverse. At the same time, their respective contexts and priority issues diverge, possibly along some key dimensions, although this is a question better addressed through greater future cooperation and discussion between the two regions' youth research scholars. For the moment, we might simply conclude that the complexity of European patterns of culture as expressed through multiple European youth research literatures is a less accessible source of knowledge for most North American specialists.

Change and Diversity in Europe

Since the 1980s, a significant rise has occurred in Europe in both the empirical range of diversity and the cultural perception of diversity within its expanding economic and political borders. The demise of the Soviet bloc and the democratic transformation of central and eastern Europe from 1989 gave, step by step, Europe back to itself. "Western" and "eastern" European societies came to recognize each other once more, beyond the schematic stereotypes of the cold war era and the memories of Europeans old enough to remember the early decades of 20th-century Europe. This alone has had a remarkable effect, not least for young people in Europe, for whom a whole new world opened up virtually overnight—and this goes in both directions, it should be underlined.

Not only European integration processes (formally represented by European Union Treaties and EU enlargements) but also the consequences of economic and cultural globalization (expressed in changing patterns of migration into Europe and through information technology, media, and commerce) have equally contributed to changing the face and the meanings of diversity. Concerns about the real or imagined prospect of cultural and political "standardization" tend to prevail in political and public debate, particularly among (older) adult citizens and commentators. However, on the whole, young people are more inclined to enjoy the variety that is available, although they typically prefer to remain on their home ground while doing so—with the exception of holidays abroad, which most wish for and many take. In effect, we begin to detect here life-phase-related (and possibly ultimately intergenerational) differences in the ways in which Europeans manage the tensions and ambiguities between national-cultural specificities and transnational commonalities.

All the points addressed so far are relevant for the modernization of youth transitions in Europe. The contributions to this collection present a set of pictures of youth in today's Europe, and each sets its picture into a common frame: (a) the diversity of national cultures and (b) traditions interacting with common problems such as new multiculturalisms as a consequence of European integration and globalization.

Three Key Dimensions of Change

In this collection, describing and analyzing the modernization of youth transitions in Europe take their cue from three key dimensions of change in young people's lives:

1. Changing relations between education, training, and the labor market: what does this mean for young people's learning and working trajectories?
2. Changing relations between the generations: what does this mean for patterns of dependence and autonomy between parents and children?
3. Changing time and space relations: what does this mean for young people's perceptions of their future lives in a world in which real-time virtual communication reaches across physical space and proximate locations can be ever-more readily exchanged for distant, unfamiliar, and yet real-life study, work, and travel experiences?

The initial driving force for the application of contemporary modernization theory in youth studies was the emergence of high youth unemployment rates after the mid-1970s, followed by structural change in the youth labor market toward a greater likelihood of vulnerable employment (part-time and temporary work, underemployment and multiple jobs, public-subsidy programs). Over time, youth transitions between schooling and employment became increasingly protracted and fragmented for higher proportions of youth cohorts. Formal education and training qualifications, hence, came to play an ever-stronger role in prefiguring life chances and risks. Gradually, higher participation rates in education and training served to postpone the labor market-entry problem, to set credential inflation into motion, and to intensify polarization processes in general. By the 1990s, it had become abundantly clear that school-to-work transitions are one element of broader modernization patterns relating to youth within the life course as a whole. This was the starting point for the kind of research reported in this volume.

Youth unemployment is a recognized problem in North America, but explicit links with the sociological analysis of contemporary modernization have not taken a prominent role in the literature; Côté (2000) and Arnett (2004) are notable recent exceptions. In Europe, on the other hand, youth researchers have developed the concept of a *new youth biography*. This term refers to the consequences of the deconstruction of standard biographies, which were based on a three-phase social life course: socially differentiated education and training; gender-differentiated work lives, founded in full and continuous employment for men and mainly family responsibilities for women; and age-defined retirement for men and continued family responsibilities for women.

Today's emerging "choice biographies" imply that whereas social origin and gender are still relevant in a range of ways, they no longer exercise the same kind of aggregate prestructuring of education, training, and employment trajectories as they used to do. Biographical individualization, which has both objective and subjective dimensions, means that social factors (class, gender, ethnic origin) impact youth in subtler and more differentiated ways. Social factors equally bring greater risks and contingencies for each and every person as an individual subject. Risk and choice are bound together through life.

NEW DIRECTIONS FOR CHILD AND ADOLESCENT DEVELOPMENT • DOI: 10.1002/cad

It is important to add that these ideas, together with the initial research that accompanied their development, originated during the 1980s in more affluent continental western Europe and the Nordic countries. They spread during the 1990s to the British Isles and Ireland (where more purely neo-Marxist approaches had held greater influence) and then to southern, central, and eastern Europe. This might well be regarded as an example of the development of discursive hegemony in European intellectual life and, furthermore, one that did not derive from the English-language theoretical literature in the first instance; rather, it derives from German-language discourse and its influence in Dutch and Nordic scientific communities.

The dynamics of European transformation and integration routinely produce tension around the dialectic of continuity and discontinuity: European polities are caught up in the turmoil; their young people experience it first hand and try to negotiate pathways through a world that those born only two or three decades earlier would have found hard to imagine in their own youth. European youth researchers, for their part, have had to work out new theoretical, methodological, and empirical approaches to deal with the panoply of old and new diversities. This is the practical context in which intercultural and comparative youth research in Europe has developed.

The YOYO and FATE Projects

The contributors to this volume all belong to this young community of European youth research. In the past decade, they have worked together in many ways, not least in a series of projects that have covered ten countries from all parts of Europe: Ireland, the United Kingdom, Denmark, the Netherlands, Germany, Bulgaria, Romania, Italy, Spain, and Portugal. As projects funded by the European Commission's Research Framework Programs, they must deliver policy-relevant findings and are intended to contribute to building a European-wide research area.

This collection draws in particular on the YOYO and FATE projects, which are both acronyms and metaphors at the same time.[1] The acronym YOYO stands for the project title Youth Policy and Participation: Potentials of Participation and Informal Learning for Young People's Transitions to the Labor Market. The acronym also connotes the child's yo-yo, which represents young people's lives swinging up and down and back and forth time and again in changing curves and rhythms through to adult life and hence no longer conforming to the standard biographical patterns described earlier. Young people's fates in transition, on the other hand, are bound up with those of their families, whose capacities to support their children during this critical period of development and change in their lives are highly diverse and subject to influences often beyond their direct control; hence, the FATE project's title: Families and Transitions in Europe.

NEW DIRECTIONS FOR CHILD AND ADOLESCENT DEVELOPMENT • DOI: 10.1002/cad

The notion of transition delineates the common conceptual anchor for these projects' research-based efforts to understand how young people in Europe approach, shape, and realize their life plans. The YOYO project researchers focused on documenting destandardized school-to-work transitions and the effects these have on youths' access to citizenship and on their motivation to continue participating in education and training in the future. The researchers surveyed how youth, education, and labor market policies succeed and fail to motivate young people for active engagement in shaping their own transitions. The results show that policy measures can enhance motivation where they explicitly foresee opportunities for individual choices and spaces for experimentation and where they include nonformal educational elements.

The FATE project investigators examined the role of family support in young people's transitions to economic, household, and personal autonomy. They placed their research in the context of reduced public benefits and subsidies for young people in most European countries together with persistently high rates of youth and adult unemployment in many countries and regions. The situation of young people in eastern versus western Europe was a priority focus in the FATE project: the transition to market economies brought momentous changes for the social organization of school-to-work transitions and family support measures in the former socialist state countries.

Contributions to This Volume

In the first contribution to this collection (Chapter 2), Lynne Chisholm sets the framework within which European youth research has developed, with reference to the European policy environment. She notes the key thematic dimensions of research agendas, offers an account of how theory and research have developed and matured since the 1990s, and draws attention to the specific methodological and professional challenges of doing European youth research. The author concludes with some reflections on how interdisciplinary youth research might respond cogently to the issues and problems of these turbulent times.

We noted earlier that extended participation in initial education and training has acted as a key intermediating factor in the modernization of youth transitions in Europe. This obviously speaks to the first key dimension of change noted earlier. Translated into active, subject-related terms, this means that learning is currently at the top of educational and political agendas across Europe and at all levels. But how should learning be conceptualized in today's fast-moving world, and what are the most promising ways to develop young people's learning potential? Sven Mørch and Manuela du Bois-Reymond in Chapter 3 argue that established ways of organizing schooling and learning are no longer appropriate or effective for emerging knowledge-based societies. Learners are reclaiming their integrity, and young people readily list their dissatisfaction with existing forms of institutional, curricular, and pedagogic provision. What kinds of new learning concepts and practices are available? The authors discuss the relationship between formal, nonformal, and informal learning and pay attention to the innovative potential of "trend-setter learners" who carve out their own learning trajectories.

Today's young people experience an extended youth characterized by risks and contingencies, quasi-autonomies, and gendered tensions and ambiguities. Individualized biographies and the embryonic emergence of a new social life phase, termed *young adulthood*, place into question whole sets of conventional expectations about what life is likely to bring about—in both the short term and the long term. Should we not suspect that their ideas about young people's futures diverge from those of people several decades older than themselves? Might we be the witnesses of a sea of change in the cultural understanding of time or of lifetimes? Carmen Leccardi (in Chapter 4) explores the concept of time and future lifetime for young adults, showing how they are inclined not to plan what is no longer susceptible to planning. In other words, she demonstrates how young people apply an immanent, ephemeral rationality to the notion of the future and its "(un)controllability." Leccardi's contribution thus focuses on the third key dimension of change: changing time and space relations.

Young Europeans in the future may experience different kinds of learning environments and processes, but it is unlikely that they will experience shorter periods of initial education and training than they do today. One of the consequences is already and will certainly continue to be that young people's economic dependence on their families and households of origin will last longer than was typically the case in the second half of 20th-century Europe. Earlier, parental households in the mass of the working population favored young single people's continuing coresidence because this brought extra income once they had moved into the labor market. Now, most young people of all social backgrounds remain at least partly financially dependent on their parents for longer periods—sometimes for much longer and well into young adulthood. This places a new burden not only on parents (and sometimes siblings and grandparents) but also on the young people themselves, who experience fragmented and partial forms of autonomy. Here we refer in particular to the second key dimension of change: that is, changing relations between the generations. Hence, Andy Biggart and Siyka Kovacheva (Chapter 5) analyze the nature and scope of the demands on and the deployment of family resources in relation to young people's needs and wishes. In doing so, they set their findings in the framework of social capital theory.

Barbara Stauber's contribution in Chapter 6 combines two key ideas that inform contemporary youth research in Europe. First, she posits that being a girl or a boy and then becoming a woman or a man have lost their traditional significance in the sense that they are no longer self-evident, unquestioned identities, roles, and practices. This is another way of approaching our third key dimension of change: changing spatial relations can also refer to the repositioning of gender relations in terms of the drift away from binary toward overlapping and contingent concepts and practices. The very term *gender* connotes the problematic quality of femininity and masculinity in today's world. In other words, these concepts have accreted multiple potential meanings and consequences for personal and social action. They have to be continually negotiated within continually changing contexts of identity and practice. Second, Stauber reminds us that the capacity and competence for negotiating identities and behaviors have to be learned. This addresses our second key dimension: changing relations between the generations from the standpoint of shifting balances between primary and secondary sources of gender socialization. Today, negotiating processes are more flexible, involve a wider range of actors, and take place through action itself, through "doing gender," and above all, in informal learning settings, both among peers and at the workplace.

Chapter 7 takes us back to the starting point of youth researchers' priority concerns—in other words, back to changing relations among education, training, and the labor market, our first key dimension of change. Using the results of the YOYO project, Andreas Walther and Wim Plug analyze the features and implications of destandardization and individualization against the background of structural change in youth labor markets.

Conclusion

Fifty years from now, it might be instructively entertaining to look back to a time when so many longstanding values and assumptions about life-course transitions between youth and adulthood underwent so much change. We predict that the sequential relations among education, training, and employment will have been transformed into more fluid and open patterns that bear no necessary correspondence with life phase. We think it likely that adulthood, as an amorphous and no longer clearly defined concept and practice, will be well on the road toward deconstruction and reconstruction in novel ways yet to be described and understood. In turn, this will certainly reflect back on the social construction of youth, and this is the point at which to bring our reflections to a close: we have, as yet, no evidence, and our theories cannot predict the future. We hope, however, that this modest contribution will foster greater cooperation between European and North American youth researchers. What would we most like our readers to carry forward with them after having made their way through this collection? There are two central ideas that we wanted this collection to convey. First, studying social and cultural diversity—here represented by contemporary Europe—is a rich source of theoretical inspiration. Second, youth as a life phase is neither an immovable feast nor an inevitable plague. It is a social and cultural construction within a historically specific phenomenon: sociologically speaking, it is time to bring youth back into the life course.

NEW DIRECTIONS FOR CHILD AND ADOLESCENT DEVELOPMENT • DOI: 10.1002/cad

Note

1. Both projects were carried out between 2001 and 2004. For the YOYO project, Walther, du Bois-Reymond, and Biggart (2006) conducted an analysis of youth work and vocational integration policy measures in combination with interviews with young people, project personnel, and other social stakeholders. For the FATE project, Biggart (2005) conducted a questionnaire survey and qualitative interviews with young people and their parents.

References

Arnett, J. J. (2004). *Emerging adulthood: The winding road from the late teens through the twenties.* New York: Oxford University Press.

Biggart, A. (2005). *Families and transitions in Europe: Final scientific report.* Coleraine, Ireland: University of Ulster.

Côté, J. E. (2000). *Arrested adulthood: The changing nature of maturity and identity.* New York: New York University Press.

Walther, A., du Bois-Reymond, M., & Biggart, A. (2006). *Participation in transition: Motivation of young people for learning and work.* Frankfurt/Berlin/Bern: Lang.

MANUELA DU BOIS-REYMOND *is professor emeritus of education and youth studies at the University of Leiden in the Netherlands. Her fields of interest concern intercultural youth and childhood studies in the fields of intergenerational relationships, youth transitions, and new forms of learning.*

LYNNE CHISHOLM *holds the chair for education and generation at the University of Innsbruck's Institute of Educational Sciences, Innsbruck, Austria, and is director of the institute. She specializes in the comparative and intercultural study of education, training, and youth, including the intersections between research, policy, and practice in these fields.*

NEW DIRECTIONS FOR CHILD AND ADOLESCENT DEVELOPMENT • DOI: 10.1002/cad

2

This chapter presents the development of European youth research as a distinctive field of study. It draws attention to the sociopolitical context in which the field has emerged, outlines the key dimensions of the field's agenda, reports on significant facets of theory and research development to date, and briefly considers the field's methodological and professional challenges.

European Youth Research: Development, Debates, Demands

Lynne Chisholm

The development of a consciously and specifically European youth research field is closely associated with the emergence during the past fifteen years or so of the following:

- A recognizable sociopolitical European-level public sphere of discourse
- The growth of relevant institutional policy action by supranational organizations
- A rising sense of contemporary Europe as a world region in the context of economic and cultural globalization processes

The societal transformation of central and eastern Europe after 1989, followed by the transition to independence of former Soviet republics in the Caucasus and central Asia, together with the restructuring of southeast Europe, added a significant dynamic to these parallel developments.

These social, political, and economic changes have led to new priorities for youth studies, both from within the research community itself and as a consequence of policy responses. The European policy level has been of particular importance in shaping the pace and direction of research priorities. This is partly because there has been an overall shift in the distribution of research budgets toward expanding the funding resources available through European Union (EU) channels in comparison with those available at national levels. Youth researchers, therefore,

NEW DIRECTIONS FOR CHILD AND ADOLESCENT DEVELOPMENT, no. 113, Fall 2006 © Wiley Periodicals, Inc.
Published online in Wiley InterScience (www.interscience.wiley.com) • DOI: 10.1002/cad.165

have considerable incentives to look for project funding beyond the borders of their national scientific communities.

Five Europe-wide research studies on the situation of young people in Europe were undertaken between 1991 and 2004 (Chisholm & Bergeret, 1991; Chisholm & Kovacheva, 2002; Orr, 2004; Schizzerotto & Gasperoni, 2000; United Nations Children's Fund/Monitoring in Central and Eastern Europe, the Commonwealth of Independent States and the Baltics, 2000). Between 1990 and 2005, six Eurobarometer (the public opinion analyses sector of the European Commission) youth surveys were conducted.[1] Some relevant research studies (including those reported in this volume) have also been funded through EU Research Framework Programs,[2] together with European Commission education and training action programs.[3] Finally, the white paper on youth (European Commission, 2001) action priorities included, for the first time, developing common objectives for a greater understanding and knowledge of youth (that is, including research-based knowledge). In the same year, the European Commission-Council of Europe Partnership Covenants on Youth Worker Training and on Youth Research was launched, which has led to regular research seminars and publications on priority topics.[4]

The sheer pace and scale of these research-related developments and outcomes convey the significance in the past 15 years of the emergence of European youth research as a specialist professional community. In this chapter, I detail the key dimensions of the field's agenda, present significant facets of theory and research development to date, and consider some of the methodological and professional challenges to be faced.

Key Dimensions of Agenda Development

The establishment of a distinctive and recognizable terrain for European youth research can be described as a process of discursive and practical reconstruction. On the one hand, youth studies have traditionally been located in several disciplines: history, psychology, sociology, education, and more recently, cultural studies.

Interdisciplinary approaches and coalitions have been gaining ground since the 1970s, more evidently at the international level (for example, within the framework of the International Sociological Association's Youth Research Committee[5]) than at the national level. For the most part, Europe's youth research communities remained largely ensconced within their own languages and academic cultures, whereas four decades of political division had engendered cultural schism between western and eastern European research communities and their respective theoretical and methodological traditions. International networks had hence become the only sites for encounter and exchange: these were the areas in which not only interdisciplinary approaches but also intercultural perspectives could be imagined and piloted. Many of those who have contributed to the development of

NEW DIRECTIONS FOR CHILD AND ADOLESCENT DEVELOPMENT • DOI: 10.1002/cad

European youth research in the past 15 years were active in international networks long before then.

On the other hand, the history of youth studies has been a rather closeted affair in the sense that its focus of attention cuts across the logic of the division of labor between specialist research and policy fields that are discursively more powerful: family, education and training, labor market and employment, health, and crime and justice. From the 1970s onwards, youth cultural studies, which originated primarily in Anglo-American academic discourse and spread rapidly to the major European youth research communities in the 1980s, had done much to lend a distinctive, more autonomous identity to youth studies as a specialist field (see Brake, 1980). The massive dislocations of the 1980s (economic restructuring and high youth unemployment in western Europe) and 1990s (political and economic transformation in central, eastern, and southeastern Europe) then brought such significant change into young people's lives and prospects that the development of new theoretical and empirical frameworks became inevitable.

At the same time, contemporary modernization theory and intense engagement with understanding the formation and transformation of subjectivity in postmodern cultures brought the individual subject under the academic gaze. In effect, this prefigured a discursive shift toward observation and analysis through time and from the standpoint of the subject or, put differently, toward the study of youth within the life course as well as youth "in and for itself."

Taken together, the features underlying the construction of European youth research as a distinctive and recognizable terrain can be summarized along the following dimensions:

- From additive to integrative perspectives and analyses
- Linking macrostructural with microcultural approaches
- Setting youth transitions into the larger life-course theory and research framework
- Focusing on the implications of macrosocial change for youth transitions
- Bringing research, policy, and practice into closer critical interrogation
- Mapping new methodological and professional challenges.

An Integrated Process of Theory-Research Development

The study of changing youth transitions has been the major theme of European youth research since the beginning of the 1990s; this section focuses on this topic but not exclusively. The anchoring feature of the process of theory and research development in European youth studies can be described as the effort to bring perspectives on and understandings of youth transitions up-to-date and to do so within the framework of making sense of great empirical complexity and in a period of rapid social change. This process incorporates a number of core thematic elements that can be approached from several different angles and that have successively shaped the overall development of youth studies in Europe.

Condensed into their essentials, these elements represent four facets of theoretical and research concern: autonomy, participation, inequality, and inclusion. Young people's access to and acquisition of autonomy translate into charting the changing patterns of transitions to adulthood. Young people's understandings and practices of participation derive from the analysis of social and political attitudes and behaviors, not only in representative democratic channels but also in everyday life. Observing and estimating the balances between chances and risks in young people's lives and future prospects—that is, studying inequalities—now gives more emphasis to region (within Europe and within countries) and to intergenerational relations (in the light of the demographic transition to aging societies). At its most general level, the extent to which young people experience economic, social, and political inclusion as citizens in their own right can be related to each of the three preceding facets of concern. More specifically, the theme of inclusion speaks to the objective recasting and the subjective reinvention of Europe as a multicultural, multilingual, and multiethnic world region, both at the macropolitical level (European cooperation and integration) and in the life worlds and identities of those who live in its cities and countrysides.

The collapse of youth labor markets that took increasing hold in 1980s western Europe brought a series of disjunctions into view. In the first place, young people in much of southern Europe had never really experienced buoyant youth labor markets, no more than had their parents and grandparents before them. Patterns of youth transitions in these settings bore limited similarity to those in more affluent northwestern Europe, but these differences had played no role at all in the development of conceptual models of youth transitions. In the second place, visible structural gaps opened up between young people's transition chances and risks in northern European countries. In both the United Kingdom and in France, youth unemployment rates had soared to persistently high levels. In continental northwestern Europe, the deterioration came more slowly and later, whereas in the Nordic countries such problems remain comparatively mild.

Training and employment opportunities for poorly qualified and unqualified young people entering the labor market for the first time deteriorated most sharply, but it also became evident that cultural and normative expectations surrounding the youth phase differed among northern European countries, and these differences were reflected in theoretical approaches on youth as a life phase (Chisholm, Büchner, Krüger, & Brown, 1990). Youth researchers in continental northwestern Europe and in the Nordic countries were particularly interested in the idea and practice of youth as a moratorium—that is, a positively constructed space for exploration and experimentation. The longer the time societies could afford to give young people for personal development and autonomous cultural practice, the better. This perspective was relatively incomprehensible for youth researchers coming from the United Kingdom and Ireland, where the idea of a positive moratorium had never taken theoretical root and did not, in any case, correspond with transition patterns for the great majority of young people.

Cultural perspectives on youth existed, however, alongside a separate tradition of largely cohort-based research into school-to-work transitions. Typically more quantitative in character, these analyses not only were able to record the gradual extension and fragmentation of pathways to economic independence but also began to document differences between countries' transitions systems (for example, Evans & Heinz, 1994). On the one hand, the conceptual confrontation between perspectives that highlight subjective autonomy and those that map systemic constraints resulted in a highly fruitful theoretical dynamic during the 1990s that worked with the structure and agency dialectic to understand new and old inequalities in youth transitions in terms of complex patterns of chances and risks (for example, Dwyer & Wyn, 2001). On the other hand, the empirical confrontation between differently structured patterns of youth transitions in western Europe as compared with central and eastern Europe (in different ways, both before and after 1989) led inescapably to the conclusion that existing models could not adequately capture the European patchwork of similarities and differences (Wallace & Kovatcheva, 1998).

Youth studies in the 1980s had documented and understood the nature and the consequences of high youth unemployment in causing delayed and extended transitions to adulthood and hence hindering or blocking personal, economic, and social autonomy. Youth researchers identified the solution in straightforward terms: reduce youth unemployment so that youth transitions can once more take their normal course. However, by the mid-1990s, it was clear that the normal course of events would not reestablish itself anywhere in Europe, whatever this had previously implied. Rather, the emerging transition to knowledge-based economies had begun to restructure the labor market, occupational profiles, and work processes, but national education and training systems had not seriously begun to adapt. By this time, young people's education and training participation rates had risen sharply everywhere (albeit from different starting points) but more in response to the problems of the youth labor market than through recognition of the need for higher level and different kinds of qualifications and competences.

Transitions to the labor market were taking place not only later but also in more differentiated and gradual ways as young people mixed study and work in a combination between practical economic necessity, tactical career planning, and personal choices. The opening up of the new Europe, both in terms of EU-based integration and in the tearing of the concrete veil between the west and the east, set its societies and cultures into motion, both physically and imaginatively. Young Europeans could now think of their lifestyles and futures in different ways; new options for realization became practically available.

The nature and direction of these kinds of changes produced, in a first step, the reconceptualization of the character and meaning of the youth phase in terms of the destandardization and individualization of youth transitions, whether constructed positively or, more worryingly, amid an almost chaotic array of old and new inequalities (Furlong & Cartmel, 1997). The feature that has engendered most concern in European youth research is the emergence— or probably more accurately, the reemergence—of a severe polarization of life chances of young people from different parts of Europe and from different social and ethnic backgrounds. These differences are increasingly mediated through education and qualification but, in addition, in a context of renewed differentiation in educational provision (especially in vocational education and training and in higher education) that reintroduces greater inequalities of access and outcome value. This is especially the case in central and eastern European countries, which have experienced rapid and extensive privatization in the education and training sector.

Furthermore, the characteristic feature of tightening links between education, qualification, and labor market integration is their negative, exclusionary quality. While low qualification levels are an increasingly sure route to long-term exclusion from employment other than at the margins of the labor market, high qualification levels alone are no sure route to employment and career, whether in the short term or in the longer term. Young people in Europe today no longer can look forward to stable and secure employment careers but more likely to continuous change throughout their active working lives—and hence to the need to participate in work-related learning on a lifelong basis. This, too, plays an increasingly important role in the ways in which young people understand the nature of life planning and future prospects as highly contingent, provisional matters, which in turn contributes to the further destandardization of youth transitions as the formation of subjectivity among younger generations adapts to new circumstances: young people come to want what they will, in any case, have to come to terms with.

In a second step, the theses of destandardization and individualization were empirically extended to cover the full range of young people's lives: not only education and work, but also family formation, lifestyle, and values (in European perspective, brought together in Chisholm & Kovacheva, 2002; Chisholm, de Lillo, Leccardi, & Richter, 2003; Schizzerotto & Gasperoni, 2000). Together with a belated recognition of the potential effects of rapid demographic change for intergenerational relations and social divisions of labor, in the past few years, theoretical interest has gradually reoriented. Youth researchers are now increasingly placing youth as a concept and practice into wider sets of social relations. On the one hand, macrotheoretical discourses on contemporary modernization in Europe insert both economic and cultural globalization processes and technological change into the framing conditions of young Europeans' lives (for example, Blossfeld, Klijzing, Mills, & Kurz, 2005; Bynner, 1998; Facer & Furlong, 2001;

Helve & Holm, 2005; Sefton-Green, 2003). On the other hand, the social reconstruction of the life course and age-linked identities and lifestyles means that it has become increasingly implausible to detach youth from other life phases, whose borders with each other and internal structuring and meaning are equally changing. Within this, discussion and debate over the emergence of a new life phase of young adulthood currently take a prominent place (Arnett, 2004, 2006; Bynner, 2005; and most contributions in this volume).

Finally, alongside these developments, European youth research has, from the outset and increasingly, given much emphasis to describing and analyzing young people's political engagement with national and European policy matters (see, for example, SORA, 2005; Spannring, Wallace, & Haerpfer, 2001; Wallace, Datler, & Spannring, 2005). This concern derives from two plainly observable phenomena. First, young Europeans—as do their elders—express widespread disillusion with and loss of trust in established channels and forums of political representation and social action. Second, they are little inclined to participate in organized civil society, including in traditional youth associations like Guiding and Scouting. Innumerable studies and surveys—including the "youth Eurobarometers" referred to in the first part of this chapter—attest to all this. They also confirm the subjective importance of contingent commitment: having the freedom to move in and out of sites of participation and involvement as and when one chooses.

At the same time, overwhelming majorities of young people throughout Europe continue to hold to values and principles that express attachment to solidarity and community, certainly in the broad sociopolitical sense and also at the local, everyday, and familiar level. Young people also express a greater degree of positive acceptance of European integration than do their elders, at least in part because they see the practical benefits in terms of wider opportunities for education, employment, choice of residence, and quite simply, mobility as adventure and excitement. Some of this is immediately explicable in terms of growing up in a more integrated and open Europe—that is, different socialization and learning experiences in comparison with their parents and grandparents. However, much remains to be researched and understood, not least with respect to changing perspectives and practices of active citizenship in complex, multilayered European societies that are only slowly rethinking democratic governance.

In reflecting on just how much young people's lives have changed since the beginning of the 1990s, European youth studies are now approaching a conceptual watershed. The normative reference points to which empirical patterns of youth transitions have been related no longer play a theoretically useful function. Standardized life-course patterns and the "normal biography" refer to economic and social worlds that with globalization and information technology have changed irrevocably: the linearities of the first modern era are mutating into the recursivities of postmodernity. The concept of coherent and stable identities that can only belong, and must always belong, to some categories of experience, identification, and representation and not to others is becoming untenable.

Finally, the paradigm shift to lifelong and life-wide (work, family, education, and leisure) learning that accompanies ongoing structural change in European labor markets, employment patterns, occupations, and work processes is already palpable in policy and practice throughout Europe's education and training systems. In the posited knowledge societies of Europe's future, the fundamental character of teaching and learning changes, not least with respect to the life phase of those expected to participate and benefit (Chisholm, 2000; other contributions to this volume). From this point of view, either all must become young or youth can no longer be specially defined as "in transition" to something else. These are the kinds of questions that European youth researchers are only just beginning to formulate.

Methodological and Professional Challenges

Youth studies belong to social research and therefore share its well-known methodological challenges. Researching youth also brings research ethics— a professional challenge—to the forefront in considering how young people can and should be informed and included as active research subjects in studies about youth. What are the particular methodological and professional challenges that arise when youth research bears the qualifying adjective "European"?

As noted earlier in this chapter, one of the key dimensions of the European youth research agenda lies in its ambition to deliver integrative perspectives and analyses. This means not only developing the conceptual capacity to produce holistic analyses of young people's lives and worldviews but also finding ways to reach across the boundaries of language, culture, and datasets to move toward genuinely intercultural analyses (Bynner & Chisholm, 1998).

In practical terms, all comparative researchers have to find ways to deal with disparate data sets. Noncongruence in patterns of linguistic-cultural understanding meets with nation-state-based logics of data collection and classification. The potential for cross-national comparison typically leaves space only for highly aggregated comparisons. Finding more sophisticated ways to work with units and levels of sampling and analysis is one important way forward (Bynner & Chisholm, 1998), all the more so because research communities that take Europe as their frame of reference perforce recognize that similarities and differences are at least as complex and illuminating within countries as between them; several contributions to this volume allude to these problems. They must try to work within a field of conceptual and analytical tension between globalization and regionalization or, put differently, in the dialectic between "bundling and unbundling."

The chapters in this volume are written in English, and all the references at the end of this chapter are English-language publications, although by no means all of them were written by first-language English speakers.

These features represent, in the first instance, a practical concern for accessibility to a North American readership. They equally reflect the European dual reality of multilingualism and discursive imbalance in research communication and exchange, including in youth research. This is of particular concern because of the significance of language as a medium for the communication and exchange of cultural meaning, in academia as in everyday life (to which the introductory chapter in this volume alludes).

Not only ethnic-cultural diversity in Europe but also the increasingly global character of communication and entertainment media introduces new and widely available sources of cultural information and knowledge into everyday life. By and large, public and political debate judges the globalization of media and markets to result in the decline of desirable cultural diversity in Europe—that is, risks the fading or adulteration of indigenous majority cultural traditions and ways of life in Europe's nation-states. Youth researchers temper this perspective by drawing attention to the ways in which young people create new, hybrid lifestyles from a variety of cultural elements that derive from different parts of Europe, different parts of the world, and different ethnic-cultural traditions.

The discursive world of European youth research is also culturally and linguistically hybrid, certainly in professional affiliation and real-time communication. The European youth studies community recognizes itself through networking, but it lacks an institutional focus at the European level (for example, through a Europe-wide dedicated research institute), and those who belong to that community work in a variety of disciplines and types of organizations. Working in this field requires competences that go beyond those needed by researchers working conventionally in their "home" academic cultures. These correspond to the new basic competences that European-level education and training policy identifies as generally important for the future: languages, social and intercultural skills, capacity for teamwork, and adaptability to change. These competences make it possible for technical research skills to be applied appropriately, and they maximize the chances of successful project outcome in multinational research groups. In addition, many of those who work in European youth studies place importance on open and participative models of research, which means that they must be able to cooperate with those working in youth policy and practice, not least with youth nongovernment organizations and, on occasion, with young people themselves. All these competences require professional training and experience, which currently few universities provide in a systematic way.

Conclusion

Having reviewed the development of the past 15 years or so, I conclude, first, that much has been achieved and, second, that the European youth research field now needs greater priority and resources to achieve consolidation. How can youth research help to develop better answers to the

NEW DIRECTIONS FOR CHILD AND ADOLESCENT DEVELOPMENT • DOI: 10.1002/cad

problems of our times? Being willing and able to answer such questions is part of the modernization of youth research in Europe, a reflection of its own coming-of-age as a recognized specialist field as well as the expression of social responsibility.

Notes

1. "Young Europeans 1990" (Special Survey 51), "Young Europeans 1997" (Eurobarometer [EB] 47.2), "Young Europeans 2001" (EB 55.1), "Attitudes and Opinions of Young People in the European Union on Drugs" (EB 57.2/Special EB 171, 2002), "Youth in New Europe" (EB 2003.1, 2003), and "Youth Takes the Floor: Young Europeans' Concerns and Expectations as to the Development of the European Union" (special publication from EB 62.1, 63, and 63.1, December 2005). Previously, two youth Eurobarometers had been carried out in 1982 (EB 17) and 1987 (Special Survey 38). The survey questions posed in 1987 and 1990 were largely comparable, as were those in 1997 and 2001. The 2002 drugs survey is a stand-alone inquiry. The 2003 "new Europe" survey selects key topics from the preceding "Young Europeans" Eurobarometers to provide comparable material for young people in the member states acceding to the EU in 2004 (central European countries, the Baltics, Cyprus, and Malta). The most recent survey report, "Youth Takes the Floor," focuses on tomorrow's Europe, active citizenship, and the Lisbon Strategy's Youth Pact. All Eurobarometer reports (except "Young Europeans 1990," which is out of print and not yet available online) are accessible at http://europa.eu.int/comm/public_opinion/archives/eb_special_en.htm.

2. Projects are accessible at http://europa.eu.int/comm/research/social-sciences/index_en.html.

3. See programs and actions at http://europa.eu.int/comm/education/index_en.html.

4. Information on events, reports, and publications is accessible at http://www.coe.int/T/E/Cultural_Co-operation/Youth/; see also http://www.training-youth.net/INTEGRATION/TY/Intro/index.html.

5. Information is accessible at http://www.alli.fi/youth/research/ibyr/index.htm.

References

Arnett, J. J. (2004). *Emerging adulthood: The winding road from the late teens through the twenties.* New York: Oxford University Press.

Arnett, J. J. (2006). Emerging adulthood in Europe: A response to Bynner. *Journal of Youth Studies, 9*(1), 111–123.

Blossfeld, H.-P., Klijzing, E., Mills, M., & Kurz, K. (Eds.) (2005). *Globalization, uncertainty, and youth in society.* London: Routledge.

Brake, M. (1980). *The sociology of youth culture and youth subcultures.* London: Routledge.

Bynner, J. (1998). Youth in the information society: Problems, prospects, and research directions. *Journal of Education Policy, 13*(3), 433–442.

Bynner, J. (2005). Rethinking the youth phase of the life-course: The case for emerging adulthood. *Journal of Youth Studies, 8*(4), 367–384.

Bynner, J., & Chisholm, L. (1998). Comparative youth transition research: Methods, meanings, and research relations. *European Sociological Review, 14*(2), 131(150.

Chisholm, L. (2000). The educational and social implications of the transition to knowledge societies. In O. von der Gablentz, O. D. Mahnke, P.-C. Padoan, & R. Picht (Eds.), *Europe 2020: Adapting to a changing world* (pp. 75–90). Baden-Baden, Germany: Nomos.

Chisholm, L., & Bergeret, J.-M. (1991). *Young people in the European community: Towards an agenda for research and policy.* Report for the Task Force Human Resources, Education, Training and Youth. Brussels: Commission of the European Communities.

Chisholm, L., Büchner, P., Krüger, H.-H., & Brown, P. (Eds.) (1990). *Childhood, youth and social change.* Lewes, UK: Falmer Press.

Chisholm, L., de Lillo, A., Leccardi, C., & Richter, R. (Eds.) (2003). *Family forms and the young generation in Europe.* European Observatory on the Social Situation, Demography and Family Annual Seminar Report. Vienna: Austrian Institute for Family Studies.

Chisholm, L., & Kovacheva, S. (2002). *Exploring the European youth mosaic: The social situation of young people in Europe.* Strasbourg: Council of Europe Publishing.

Dwyer, P., & Wyn, J. (2001). *Youth, education, and risk: Facing the future.* London: Routledge/Falmer.

Evans, K., & Heinz, W. R. (1994). *Becoming adults in England and Germany.* London/Bonn: Anglo-German Foundation.

European Commission White Paper (2001). *A new impetus for European youth.* Brussels: European Commission.

Facer, K., & Furlong, R. (2001). Beyond the myth of the "cyberkind": Young people at the margins of the Information Revolution. *Journal of Youth Studies, 4*(4), 451–469.

Furlong, A., & Cartmel, F. (1997). *Young people and social change: Individualization and risk in late modernity.* Buckingham, U.K.: Open University Press.

Helve, H., & Holm, G. (Eds.) (2005). *Contemporary youth research: Local expressions and global connections.* London: Ashgate.

Orr, K. (Ed.) (2004). Education, employment and young people in Europe. *European Youth Forum Youth Report* [Electronic format]. Retrieved June 27, 2006, from http://www.youthforum.org/en/ publications/index.html.

Schizzerotto, A., & Gasperoni, G. (Eds.) (2000). *Study on the state of young people and youth policy in Europe: Report* [Electronic version]. Brussels: European Commission, Directorate General Education and Culture [subsequently published by Istituto IARD, Milan]. Retrieved June 27, 2006, from http://ec.europa.eu/youth/doc/studies/iard/summaries_en.pdf.

Sefton-Green, J. (Ed.) (2003). *Digital diversions: Youth culture in the age of multimedia.* London: Routledge.

SORA (Institute for Social Research and Analysis) (2005). *Political participation of young people in Europe: Development of indicators for comparative research in the European Union (EUYOUPART).* Final comparative report [Electronic version]. Vienna: Institute for Social Research and Analysis. Retrieved June 27, 2006, from http://www.sora.at/images/doku/euyoupart_finalcomparativereport.pdf.

Spannring, R., Wallace, C., & Haerpfer, C. (2001). Civic participation among young people in Europe. In H. Helve & C. Wallace (Eds.) *Youth, citizenship and empowerment* (pp. 32–38). Aldershot, UK: Ashgate.

United Nations Children's Fund/Monitoring in Central and Eastern Europe, the Commonwealth of Independent States and the Baltics. (2000). *Young people in changing societies.* Regional monitoring report 7. Florence: UNICEF Innocenti Research Centre.

Wallace, C., Datler, G., & Spannring, R. (2005). Young people and European citizenship. *Sociological Series* 68, Vienna: Institute for Advanced Studies.

Wallace, C., & Kovatcheva, S. (1998). *Youth in society: The construction and deconstruction of youth in East and West Europe.* London: Macmillan.

LYNNE CHISHOLM *holds the chair for education and generation at the University of Innsbruck's Institute of Educational Sciences, Innsbruck, Austria, and is director of the institute. She specializes in the comparative and intercultural study of education, training, and youth, including the intersections between research, policy, and practice in these fields.*

3

The authors deal with changes in the relationship between education and learners due to modernization processes. The motivation of the learner has become a prime force to ensure the acquisition of knowledge. That implies a broadening of educational strategies, including nonformal education to remotivate frustrated learners.

Learning in Times of Modernization

Sven Mørch, Manuela du Bois-Reymond

European educational systems are undergoing extensive changes. More young people are participating in education for longer periods. Schooling has become popular both in political planning and in everyday life. Youth life today includes all young people in education and learning. Parents are now more engaged than ever in their children's educational performance and educational perspectives; new educational practices are tried out and discussed in the educational community and are hotly debated in public media. Former apprenticeship on the work floor is replaced by formal vocational education, and even nonskilled jobs demand at least basic formal education and skills. In short, education institutionalizes all types of daily practices of young people; learning and knowledge acquisition have become a must. In the course of this development, educational systems have become both more differentiated and more integrated.

The concept of a knowledge society points to a normative aspect: in the international competition, Europe sees itself as the most competitive continent of the future. The Lisbon summit of 2000, when this ambition was claimed, pointed to new educational challenges to be met. And the Programme for International Student Assessment (PISA) studies were consequently used as arguments for changing national educational policies and local school practices (Goldstein, 2004). In Denmark, for example, an evaluation-and-test culture already in primary school is planned that was up to then unknown.

A knowledge society also points to new mechanisms of social integration. As a program, it envisions a society built on "knowledge solidarity" in

a Durkheimian sense. Knowledge as a specific form of cultural capital influences individual life perspectives and at the same time has become a new catalyst for social integration. In this way, it makes young people the basic actors of (post)modern society. Youth as an objective and subjective social category is constructed by educational participation. But inasmuch as knowledge is growing all the time and creates a need for lifelong learning, it also changes the role and status of youth.

Paradoxically, the very concept of knowledge challenges traditional understandings of what knowledge is and why it is needed. Knowledge, of course, is and will remain important, but the rise of the concept of competence points to redefinitions of knowledge and learning. Therefore, both the development of youth and knowledge and the role of learning and competence in late modern European societies seem to be important to understand in all their ramifications and in the lives of young people. Our contribution deals with these developments and challenges both in systemic and individual perspectives.

Three Educational Challenges

The educational perspective and especially the institutional engagement in learning are influenced by three complex processes: modernization, globalization, and individualization. Although these processes are interrelated, they carry different messages about education and learning and establish different trajectories for young people to engage in.

Modernization as a multilevel process refers to many institutional changes taking place in productive, political, and educational life. In productive life, we talk about the postindustrial society, which is characterized by information, digitalization, and computerization of productive, administrative, and social processes. In political life, new forms of democratic development have become the focus of late-modern policies, especially concerning individual rights. The notion of a "European citizen" refers to this new awareness. As to educational life, the knowledge society is on the rise and leads to two contradictory processes: democratization, which is supposed to give equal learning opportunities for all citizens, and qualification, which must differentiate student populations according to labor market demands and future professional perspectives. The practical solution to these oppositions is seen in creating a world of learning with many options for young people to choose. The more varied the educational system becomes, the more accessible it is to all young people and adaptable to changing job demands. At the same time, however, the system leads to a special challenge for young people. They are supposed to maneuver in an educational world in which a destandardization of formal trajectories (see also Chapter Seven, by Walther & Plug) makes the individual responsible for his or her educational success or failure. Educational systems on their part are challenged by the new educational expectations of their clients and for giving up traditional knowledge and teaching.

Globalization refers to an understanding of the modern world as becoming "global": the local and the global meld together and the local becomes global and the global local. All parts of the world become dependent on each other. Not only people but also production can move around in the world. Globalization, however, does not guarantee global equality, maybe the opposite. It makes all the world part of the same competing market. Globalization also influences local developments. Different levels of industrialization, salaries, and living costs in different parts of the world in tandem with unforeseen demographic developments challenge the leading position of western societies. This situation creates local awareness of global competition and the value of higher education and highly educated young people in Europe. Globalization, therefore, supports youth learning and equality and at the same time creates competition and differentiation among young people, both globally and locally. Globalization also challenges traditional perspectives on qualifications. Big international firms like Microsoft regard active engagement and being able to solve problems as more important than specific qualifications.

Individualization as such is not new, but it is changing in meaning. Individualization is about individual answers to societal developments, especially with regard to learning. It refers to which competencies individuals must develop to function in society and especially in late-modern knowledge societies. This change can be summarized as a shift from a "modern" to a "late-modern" mode of individualization (Andersen & Mørch, 2005). In modern individualization, it was important to develop a political and professional personality that was adapted to society: people should learn the rules and live by them (Giddens, 1991). This mode of individualization emerged among the bourgeoisie and in the course of industrialization spread to the working population. In particular, the educational system promoted and controlled this development.

In late modernity, the person exists as, and the individualization process is more focused on, a private individual who is, or should be, related to society. Individuality today is no longer seen as the result of a socialization process but as the prerequisite for a never-ending process of personal development. Therefore, individualization is no longer the goal in the work of social institutions and socialization steered by adults. Today it is the personal qualities of individuals that count. These changes have followed a broad societal trend: a greater awareness of and engagement in children's life perspectives and individual rights.

Late-modern societies seem to be caught in the predicament of how to secure broad social interests at the same time that the individual and subjectivity are made the prerequisite of activity. One answer is that children and young people must learn to solve problems themselves. As Baumann (1991) writes, societal problems today should be solved in individual biography. It is in the individual's interest to find a way into society, to get an education and later a job. Therefore, a popular answer in education to the posed question is to work on children's motivation and to induce the principle of "responsibility for own learning." Another answer to this new mode of individualization is to develop new forms of social integration. Here participation and democratization become the leading perspectives alongside new forms of learning; nonformal learning becomes an option.

However, the new learning is not without problems. Young people may become disengaged from school life, give up learning ambitions, or leave the educational system altogether. They then experience a "relative deindividualization." They may be in danger of not obtaining the competencies needed to perform as citizens and professionals in late-modern society.

To reflect the late-modern learning perspective, it may be helpful to distinguish between the three aspects of "being, knowing, and doing" (Mørch, 2003). In the classic school of the 19th century, the being dimension was seen as most important in education. Young bourgeois, besides good manners, should learn the classics, Latin, and Greek and be molded into educated persons to fulfill their future social positions. Today the being dimension points to a more private or individualized part of the personality, meaning a certain kind of identity or self-understanding.

Around the end of the 19th century, the knowing dimension became central. Industrialization demanded qualifications: skills and knowledge became important. Education became mass education, albeit with different curricula for the upper and the lower classes. In contrast to the knowing dimension of school life, the doing dimension was developed in everyday life and in the apprenticeship model. It focused on the development of skills. "Doing" was something that happened in real working life. In this way, school knowledge and practical skills were opposites that must be bound together as different forms of learning.

Today it seems as if the doing dimension has become a new challenge and a basic ingredient of learning without the value of being and knowing declining. The discussions around the issue of competence ask the question of "doing late modernity." For individuals, this means that they should be able to understand what they (should) do. They must understand late-modernity demands, but they also need "being" self-confidence and "knowing" knowledge.

Institutionalized Individualization and Individualized Learning

Educational systems have developed different models for individualization. If we see them as "plans of individualization," we may experience how they form the trajectories and biographical challenges of individualization and individualized learning. Although some basic similarities exist, the educational systems in western European societies also show differences that have less to do with the level of knowledge and technology and more with the way education is socially distributed according to demands for equality in education.

The model of differentiated qualification reproduces social background in educational contexts. It was developed in 19th-century Europe, when young people were expected to take over the parental occupation and social status. The school system sorted children at the school gate. Some would have a learning biography, and many would not.

Today this class reproductive system no longer exists in its pure form. Most modern education models are democratic in the sense that they emphasize the principle that all children should be given the same educational opportunities. However, inside many modern educational systems, a private school system often develops that gives special opportunities to children from upper social backgrounds.

A model of educational differentiation seems to have been the ordinary developmental model of education in the 20th century. It can be seen as a productive school system focused on transferring knowledge to the students. Here all children are allowed into the same school system, but inside the school they are divided into different tracks according to school performance or abstract qualifications. We may say that the school system is one dimensional. It creates one "best" educational trajectory while creating its opposite: a sorting-out process. Young people within this system are differentiated according to their individual school performance. They become engaged or disengaged according to their school success. The system solves the problem of distributing student populations according to both social class and individual performance through the content of curricula and school life morals that are in accordance with bourgeois or middle-class social values and experiences; children from a bourgeois background manage better in school than those from lower social classes, as Bourdieu and Passeron (1977) and many other scholars since then have demonstrated.

Today a third model of education has developed that could be described as a system of qualified differentiation, one that supports the individual students' learning activities. Here also, all students are part of the same educational system, but they are given different qualification perspectives according to their own interests and abilities. This model is expected to reengage the disengaged and help young people select their own trajectory in further education and position in the labor market. Therefore, various educational trajectories have been developed. In Denmark, as in many other European countries—albeit with different emphasis on equality—this system has been introduced in the postwar decades and is seen as a democratic system that should break down social class differences and guarantee "equality through education." Within this system, all students have the same opportunities, and all trajectories are seen as equally important. Depending on individual abilities, young people may follow different trajectories in education. The educational system should no longer form "normal trajectories" but function as an opportunity for developing different school or learning curricula. Young people should be taught and should learn according to their individual abilities (Wenger,

1998). An interesting consequence of this educational model seems to be that it gives room to a youth trajectory perspective. Breaking the normal trajectory, it provides opportunities for individual routes in life (Illeris, 2003). Young people have the opportunity to choose; they may even decide to give up educational trajectories and shift in and out of jobs and education for some years. A problem of this system seems to be that it is built on individual motivation (Heckhausen, 2000); young people may lack motivation and give up education.

The fourth model, the labor market-governed education system, is not based on (the ideology of) individual choice but on labor market demands. This model has been formulated mainly as a critique of the existing individualized systems. It proposes planning of individual development according to actual job situations and makes employability the basic issue (Mørch & Stalder, 2003). Of course, such a system has its strengths and weaknesses. On the one hand, it may become static—as it was in former socialist countries—and not be able to develop new competencies for the future. Or it may create educational trajectories that are unpopular among young people and therefore unsuccessful.

The challenge of educational systems today seems to be to find a new model or logic that solves the problem of competence versus knowledge at an institutional as well as an individual level.

Education as a societal issue points to institutionalized individualization. At the same time, education also creates individual trajectories and biographies. Individual individualization is not only the answer to institutional individualization, it is also the result of individual biographical development (Mørch, 1999). And the process of individualization in biography is most sensitive to individual experiences in educational contexts. That is to say, it seems necessary to construct a new meeting point between educational individualization and the demands of late-modern labor market individualization. Educational systems and the labor market must develop a common understanding of late-modern competencies, a model of "fields of competence" (Mørch, 2003). Fields of competence should point not only to information technology but also to esthetical, personal, and social competencies. Discussion has to be launched to find out which competencies are expected from a flexible labor market and which personal competencies are needed in late-modern social and educational life. Negotiating fields of competence seems to be the new challenge everywhere.

At the level of individual individualization, the task of education systems will be to focus on the relationship among key competencies, individual practice, and biographical development. Education will have to offer trajectories that allow for choices within both an individual perspective and educational trajectories. School itself must not only modernize its traditional curriculum but also broaden it by nonformal learning practices that lead to employability, finding new ways of planning and supporting individual learning biographies (Colley, 2005; du Bois-Reymond, 2005).

NEW DIRECTIONS FOR CHILD AND ADOLESCENT DEVELOPMENT • DOI: 10.1002/cad

Learning Biographies

Whereas in earlier times—not more than one or two generations ago—school learning was regarded by the young as inevitable (though perhaps boring) and useful "for later," ever more of today's learners ask themselves what school learning is good for. They may not be able to give thorough theoretical answers, as educational scholars can, but they do have a notion, if blurred, that they live in a risk society without certainty that "everything will work out fine" in their future lives. Learning, they know, is a must: you will be nobody without a diploma; but they doubt that the official curriculum in vocational and higher education will give them what they need, now and for later.

This feeling of frustration not only has a subjective side to it, there is also hard evidence that formal education leads growing numbers of young people right into unemployment. In 2003, almost one in five of those younger than 25 years was registered as unemployed in the European Union as a whole (25 member states), rising to twice this level in Poland, for example (European Commission, 2004; and see chapter 7). Young people are, indeed, caught between the demands of institutionalized individualization and their own biographical needs and desires. The term *learning biography* refers, first, to individual persons and their experiences with education in the course of their lives; second, it refers to the different contexts within which learning takes place (Bloomer & Hodkinson, 2000; Field & Leicester, 2000). As we have shown in the previous sections, western-type societies are characterized by a high degree of institutionalized individualization, and whereas many learners still pass through the educational system without too much trouble and frustrations, many others feel out of step with the system in relation to what they want and to their identity work so far (Bynner, 2006).

Ideally speaking, we encounter two types of learners: one that represents the frustrated learner who disengages from the educational system altogether; those are early school leavers or badly performing pupils and students. The other type is represented by "productive learners" who compensate missing challenges in the school with more stimulating and self-chosen activities outside it, with the majority of learners to be found in varying numbers somewhere in between these two types. As educational innovation discourses tell us, all learners need more individualized educational methods and approaches. But whereas disengaged learners must be prevented from falling out of the educational boat or must be helped to reenter it through all kinds of compensatory and training programs, the other group, the productive learners, are recognized as incorporating human capital that is underused by formal education and must be exploited better through enriched curricula to respond to the new demands of knowledge societies.

In what follows, we discuss conditions and constellations under which productive learning occurs and how learning biographies are written. We start from the notion that what productive learners do and achieve fits the knowledge-based society better than what existing education and work

NEW DIRECTIONS FOR CHILD AND ADOLESCENT DEVELOPMENT • DOI: 10.1002/cad

organizations have to offer. We ask if the biographies of productive learners embody a new cultural script for late-modern societies.

Remotivating Disengaged Learners

In the YOYO project (see Chapter 1; Walther, du Bois-Reymond, & Biggart, 2006), we studied young people whose learning biographies had been unsuccessful and who, therefore, were in danger of becoming socially marginalized (see Chapter 7). Regular school and working careers did not reach them anymore. Therefore, we were interested in case studies that were especially designed for these kinds of frustrated learners. These were cases in the fields of youth and community work as well as preparatory measures to facilitate labor market integration. All these different projects had one thing in common: they were based on the philosophy that remotivation of frustrated learners depended on giving them the opportunity to exert influence on their own learning environment and thus their biography. When we had observed them through the various projects for one year, we discovered that many of them had appropriated the attitudes of productive learners during that year. We singled out several constellations and conditions that accounted for that success, and we will discuss now how they relate to each other.

One of the biggest problems of disengaged and frustrated learners is that their life course so far is marked by an accumulation of failures, not only in one area or at one point in time, but successively and in many different life areas. By the time they leave education and have failed to find a satisfactory job or profession, their self-esteem has been bruised, and they have lost trust in institutional help. Therefore, the projects for the most disadvantaged young people created a learning and living sphere that gave the clients room and resources to assess not their weak but their strong points (du Bois-Reymond & Stauber, 2005). It was not only, and often not even mainly, the official trainers and mentors who helped them with that, but also peers who had similar experiences. Peer learning and peer support in protected environments, and with sympathetic professionals in the background, proved to be a main success factor to overcome educational dislike and discouragement in one's own capacities.

When the disengaged learners were asked about their educational experiences, many answered by pointing to two features of school that they criticized. One was the indifference of the institution with the individuality of the student ("you are but a number"); the other was the irrelevance of the content of what curricula offered them ("what is this good for anyhow?"). Both these criticisms raise precisely the dilemma of mass education in postmodern knowledge societies: it is unable to satisfy the present and immediate needs of the students, which would imply flexible curricula and combinations of nonformal with formal education. As concerns the relationship between student and teacher, education fails to respond to the changed conditions under which the socialization and the life of contemporary children take place. Students experience the discrepancy between their personality and how they interact with adults outside school with how they are perceived and treated inside school as clearly in favor of outside school life, even if that leads to failure. Students today—not only the "failures"—despise hierarchical and highly formalized relationships and look for relaxed and informal ones instead. What they yearn for but find only as rare exceptions are stimulating and encouraging adults who care for their present situation and their personal needs and desires.

The YOYO projects, different as they were, all shared the feature that they invited the young persons to develop an active attitude toward the program and thereby to exert influence on their own learning biography. We found a precarious relationship between participation, motivation, and biographically relevant learning: if one of these links is weak, the chain will break sooner or later. For disengaged young people, their learning chain at school broke because they found no way to influence their learning environment favorably to their needs, and they lost or never acquired motivation to learn the formal curriculum because they did not feel that it mattered, either to themselves or to society at large.

Let us give one example from our research for illustration: it concerns a case in Lisbon, where migration youth is given the opportunity to participate in a project that qualifies them for professional dancing performances, using their high "body motivation" to express what they are capable of. They learn and live with peers of various ages; the younger learn informally from the older participants. At the same time, they are urged by the project professionals to attend secondary education and get a diploma. They do so because they have experienced that there is a social and physical space that they may occupy to develop their learning biographies in more than one direction. This project successfully combines formal with nonformal and informal education and establishes a stable "learning chain" (for an extended account, see Walther et al., 2006).

A New Cultural Script for Knowledge Societies

As both the YOYO project and a separate Dutch study show (Diepstraten, du Bois-Reymond, & Vinken, 2006), productive learners regard learning as their biographical project, which might—but often does not—follow the institutional logic of existing education and work organizations. They have in common a high degree of reflexivity as analyzed by Giddens (1991), Baumann (1991), Beck, Giddens, and Lash (1994), and many other theorists as a new quality of life in postmodern societies. Reflecting on one's life is, of course, no new property of such societies; intellectuals have always done so. But today reflexivity is not alone a personality trait but is inherent in societal structures as well. Institutional reflexivity and individual reflexivity influence each other and thereby change all involved relationships: those between persons, between institutions, and between persons and institutions.

NEW DIRECTIONS FOR CHILD AND ADOLESCENT DEVELOPMENT • DOI: 10.1002/cad

Changing relationships between persons involve those between learners, inside and outside institutions, and between the generations. When we asked the productive learners—in the YOYO study, we called them "biographical trendsetters"—to reflect on their learning and working biographies, they gave us ample evidence of their capacity to link their own career to those of colearners, peers, as well as adults. They deliberately associated with contemporaries who searched after similar experiences of "flow" (Csikszentmihalyi, 1975) and formed loose networks (Wuthnow, 1998) to collectively explore new projects, find persons to learn from, use existing resources, and explore new ones. Learning and working for biographical trendsetters is not an activity based on predefined individual competences but is much more an enterprise that is undertaken by people who feel the same way and are ready to combine their specific know-how to make the project in question work. Within such networks, competence is not bound to competition. In that sense, these young adults are forerunners of knowledge societies that operate in a globalized world where innovative knowledge production can be achieved only through cooperation and nonhierarchical differentiation. Part of that new attitude about knowledge production is a way of thinking: not, as modernity since the Enlightenment implied and as it is still incorporated in mass schooling, in either-or categories and resolutions, but rather in and-and possibilities.

Although biographical trendsetters learn and work more with peers of their own generation, they discard the rigid demarcations between young learners and old professionals. They do not care from whom to learn, as long as there is something interesting to learn. By and large, they find school boring, but almost all told us about one exceptional teacher who had passion for his or her subject and who knew how to instill passion in his or her students. It is noteworthy that our disengaged young people told us the same. This brings us to our second point, discussed in the next section.

Changing Relationships Between Persons and Institutions

The two main institutions that relate to learning and working are schools and labor markets. As we show throughout this volume, both are not linked as reliably to each other anymore as they were in the time of high modernity, which produced gender-normal biographies. Today the biggest—and ever more acknowledged—problem of education is that it does not prepare all students for entry in the world of work, and the biggest problem of post-Fordist labor markets is that they cannot absorb all ex-school learners, especially not those with little educational capital.

To this situation, biographical trendsetters react with two main strategies: they not only look for knowledge acquisition of formal education but use old and new learning sites and resources in all kinds of combinations, thus overcoming antiquated features of formal education. Second, they design their own working careers that serve their needs and desires better

NEW DIRECTIONS FOR CHILD AND ADOLESCENT DEVELOPMENT • DOI: 10.1002/cad

than jobs in highly formalized and hierarchically structured organizations that do not allow persons to develop their capacities to the full and in a self-chosen way.

Today, not only biographical trendsetters but a majority of young people apply a step-by-step decision strategy to move on in their lives: no grand plans for the future concerning either their educational or their working trajectories; they follow a trial-and-error approach, and they adjust to newly risen situations, be those in their private lives or in their study and working careers (see also Chapter 4). But whereas the disengaged do so with a feeling of helplessness and often even revolt against officials, the biographical trendsetters do it in full consciousness because they know (and can express that knowledge, for example, in interviews but also in their extensive communications with their network mates) that it is impossible to calculate the future.

Changes in personal and institutional relationships are widely discussed in youth sociological and education innovation discourses. Evaluating what they have contributed to the problems of learning in knowledge societies, we find that the youth sociological discourse has more to offer than the education innovation discourse because it points much more urgently than the latter to the immensely grown meaning of the biographical dimension that is involved and cannot any longer be neglected in learning matters. Both discourses are united, though, in their concern with the disengaged, discriminated, underprivileged, marginalized, and socially excluded youth—in short, the NEET group, that is, those *not* in *e*ducation, *e*mployment, or *t*raining (Maguire & Rennison, 2005).

Coming back to the question of whether the new learners—be they biographical trendsetters from the start or formerly disengaged learners who have been remotivated through participatory projects—represent a new cultural script for knowledge societies, we must be cautious with an unequivocal answer. Yes, there will be more individualized learning in the future, and yes, it is more than likely that schools will adapt to new learning modes. But there is also much reason in European educational settings to signal a growing cleavage between the winning and the losing group of learners in knowledge societies.

Conclusion

In our contribution, we have drawn attention to a new relationship between the individual learner and the demands of education and learning in a knowledge-based society. We have shown that a learning chain must be developed by the educational system and the student to yield good learning results. We have also shown that the connection between individual motivation and the educational system was much looser in premodern and modern times. All the more important it becomes today to remotivate young people who have fallen off the educational track; blue collar work is no option anymore for a stable life course.

NEW DIRECTIONS FOR CHILD AND ADOLESCENT DEVELOPMENT • DOI: 10.1002/cad

Looking to educational politics, all this means that learning plans for young people must be developed—by the institution as well as by themselves—to establish valid learning biographies. But even so, with labor markets changing all the time and changing in arbitrary ways, young people are faced with an uncertain future. Therefore, learning to deal with the contingencies of late-modern societies is, and must become, part of learning biographies. The clarification of late-modern fields of competencies should be the result of ongoing discussions between all participants in educational relations and practices, formal as well as nonformal and informal ones.

References

Andersen, H., & Mørch, S. (2005). The challenged subject: Identity. *International Journal of Theory and Research, 5(3)*, 261–285.

Baumann, Z. (1991). *Modernity and ambivalence.* Cambridge, U.K.: Polity Press.

Beck, U., Giddens, A., & Lash, S. (1994). *Reflexive modernization.* Stanford, CA: Stanford University Press.

Bloomer, M., & Hodkinson, P. (2000). Learning careers: Continuity and change in young people's dispositions to learning. *British Educational Research Journal, 26(5)*, 528–597.

Bourdieu, P., & Passeron, J.-C. (1977). *Reproduction in education, society and culture.* London: Sage.

Bynner, J. (2006). Rethinking the youth phase of the life-course: The case for emerging adulthood. *Journal of Youth Studies, 8(4)*, 367–384.

Colley, H. (2005). Formal and informal models of mentoring for young people: Issues for democratic and emancipatory practice. In L. Chisholm & B. Hoskins with C. Glahn (Eds.), *Trading up: Potential and performance in non-formal learning* (pp. 31–35). Strasbourg: Council of Europe Publications.

Csikszentmihalyi, M. (1975). *Beyond boredom and anxiety.* San Francisco: Jossey-Bass.

Diepstraten, I., du Bois-Reymond, M., & Vinken, H. (2006). Trendsetting learning biographies: Concepts of navigating through late modern life. *Journal of Youth Studies, 9(2)*, 175–193.

du Bois-Reymond, M. (2005). What does learning mean in the "learning society"? In L. Chisholm & B. Hoskins with C. Glahn (Eds.), *Trading up: Potential and performance in non-formal learning* (pp. 19–26). Strasbourg: Council of Europe Publications.

du Bois-Reymond, M., & Stauber, B. (2005). Biographical turning points in young people's transitions to work across Europe. In H. Helve & G. Holm (Eds.), *Contemporary youth research: Local expressions and global connections* (pp. 63–75). Aldershot, U.K.: Ashgate.

European Commission (2004). *Social agenda: Magazine on employment and social affairs.* Luxembourg: Office for Official Publications of the European Communities.

Field, J., & Leicester, M. (2000). *Lifelong learning: Education across the lifespan.* London: Routledge/Falmer.

Giddens, A. (1991). *Modernity and self-identity: Self and society in the late modern age.* Cambridge, U.K.: Polity Press.

Goldstein, H. A. (2004). International comparisons of student attainment: Some issues arising from the PISA study. *Assessment in education: Principles, policy and practice, 11(3)*, 319–330.

Heckhausen, J. (2000). *Motivational psychology of human development.* Amsterdam: Elsevier.

Illeris, K. (2003). Learning, identity and self-orientation in youth. *Young, 11(4)*, 357–376.

Maguire, S., & Rennison, J. (2005). Two years on: The destinations of young people who are not in education, employment or training at 16. *Journal of Youth Studies, 8(2)*, 187–201.

Mørch, S. (1999). Informal learning and social contexts: The case of peer education. In A. Walther & B. Stauber (Eds.), *Lifelong learning in Europe, Vol. 2. Differences and divisions: Strategies of social integration and individual learning biographies* (pp. 135–165). Tübingen, Germany: Neuling.
Mørch, S. (2003). Youth and education. *Young, 11(1)*, 49–73.
Mørch, S., & Stalder, B. (2003). Competence and employability. In A. Blasco Lopez, W. McNeish, & A. Walther (Eds.), *Young people and contradictions of inclusion: Towards integrated transition policies in Europe* (pp. 205–222). Bristol: Polity Press.
Walther, A., du Bois-Reymond, M., & Biggart, A. (Eds.) (2006). *Participation in transition*. Frankfurt am Main: Lang.
Wenger, E. (1998). *Communities of practice: Learning, meaning and identity*. Cambridge, U.K.: Cambridge University Press.
Wuthnow, R. (1998). *Loose connections: Joining together in America's fragmented communities*. Cambridge, MA: Harvard University Press.

SVEN MØRCH is associate professor of social psychology at the University of Copenhagen. His current research focuses on youth development and late-modern challenges of individualization.

MANUELA DU BOIS-REYMOND is professor emeritus for education and youth studies at the University of Leiden in the Netherlands. Her fields of interest concern intercultural youth and childhood studies in the fields of intergenerational relationships, youth transitions, and new forms of learning.

The author connects the changing meanings of youth in contemporary western societies with the transformations in the representation of the future. The new youthful biographical constructions can be considered a central outcome of these parallel changes: they avoid long-term commitments and structure themselves around the idea of changeability.

Redefining the Future: Youthful Biographical Constructions in the 21st Century

Carmen Leccardi

If in the "first modernity" the meaning of future was construed as a time of experimentation and possibilities, in the "second modernity" it is defined rather as an uncertain dimension, as a potential limit rather than as a resource. This new semantic framework also deeply shapes the ways and forms in which young people's biographies come to be defined. These forms of temporalization do not imply, however, the pure and simple loss of the future or the giving up of a plan altogether. Rather, as recent research would indicate, at least a part of the world of young people appears to be actively involved in constructing forms of mediation between the need for subjective control over future time and the heavily risky and uncertain social environment of our days.

The mechanism called *delayed gratification*—the repression of hedonist impulses, a determination to postpone to a later date the possible satisfaction that the present can guarantee for the benefits that this postponement makes possible—is the basis of modern socialization processes. If we consider youth a biographical stage of preparation for adult life, gratification deferral looks like the keystone guaranteeing success. From this perspective, in fact, it is the ability to live the present on the basis of the future, using everyday time as an essential tool for realizing projects—and therefore sacrificing the "expressive" aspects of action in favor of the instrumental—that enables the transition process to have a positive outcome. Here the present

is not only a bridge between past and future but also the dimension that prepares for the future. Thanks to the positive relation with the present, the youth period can be represented as a time of actively awaiting adulthood (Cavalli, 1980). As a consequence, identity is constructed around a projection of self further ahead in time, thanks to which frustration accompanying present experiences can be tolerated. So if the future is considered the dimension containing the meaning of action, if it is represented as the strategic time for self-construction and the vehicle through which individual biographical narrative takes shape (Rampazi, 1985), then gratification postponement can be accepted.

In this perspective, the future is by definition the space for constructing a *life plan* and also for defining oneself: while planning what one will do in the future, one also plans in parallel who one will be. In substance, the biographical perspective that delayed gratification refers to the presence of an extended temporal horizon, a strong capacity for self-control, a conduction of life in which programming time is crucial: all these traits taken together are typical of the modern conception of individuality. We need to ask ourselves if, and to what extent, the relationship between project, biographical time, and identity that delayed gratification presupposes can still be considered valid in a social climate, like the contemporary one, in which uncertainty tends to dominate and where experiences of contingency increase (Baumann, 1995, 2000; Beck, 1999; Leccardi, 2005a). When, in fact, uncertainty increases beyond a certain point and is associated not only with the future but also with day-to-day reality, putting in question the taken-for-granted dimension, then the basis of the life plan is removed. Furthermore, whenever change, as in our day, is extraordinarily accelerated, dynamism and performance capacity are seen as imperative, and immediacy is a parameter for evaluating the quality of an act, then investing in the long-term future can seem as senseless as postponing satisfaction. Instead of relinquishing the gratifications the present can offer, it appears more sensible to train oneself to "capture the moment," keep doors open to the unexpected, and be mentally amenable to an indefiniteness that could be loaded with potential.

In this compressed temporal horizon, desires and needs structure themselves around the present: the "good life" is no longer based on long-term commitments, and ideas of stability and control lose value (Rosa, 2003). A constant opening to the possible takes the place, as a new virtue, of faithfulness to oneself. Even the notion of one's own individuality changes. In this framework, we are far from the Tocqueville-esque "reflective and tranquil" feeling that allows each person to consider himself or herself separate from fellow citizens and yet feel tied to them in a shared belonging to democratic institutions (de Tocqueville, 1835–1840/1966). Rather, the feeling of individuality spurs one to assume responsibility for "not missing the boat," as expressed through a need to explore—appropriately and at the speed required by the new century's pace—the map of one's existential priorities, making adequate biographical decisions step by step. Fundamental in this

NEW DIRECTIONS FOR CHILD AND ADOLESCENT DEVELOPMENT • DOI: 10.1002/cad

framework appears to be the ability to construct cognitive strategies that can guarantee control over time of life despite increased contingency.

To adequately comprehend the depth of these transformations, I will concentrate attention on the new accents and semantic traits that characterize the dimension of the future, taking care to clarify the changes in meaning that have affected the concept of future in these past decades. I will then discuss contemporary transformations as a way of conceptualizing youth's course of life and biographical projects. And, using the results of recent Italian research into the relationship between youth and time experience in which I was personally involved (summarized in Crespi, 2005),[1] I will analyze some of the new ways in which young people make plans. As it will be shown, these changes appear to be the result of the upheaval in conceiving of youth as a transition phase to adulthood and in the delayed-gratifications mechanism at its base and, in parallel, indicators of the "lifestyle individualization" underlying the contemporary processes of biographical construction (Beck & Beck-Gernsheim, 2003).

Second Modernity, Global Risks, and Future Crisis

In agreement with the analytical proposal of Beck (1999), we can define first modernity as the period starting with industrial modernity, which was dominated by the reality of the nation-state and in which the winning logic was that of progress interwoven with the idea of control (in the first place, over nature). In it, identity and social roles were closely intertwined. The second modernity, contemporary modernity, child of successful modernization, instead seems to be increasingly governed by processes like the intensification of globalization and global markets, a pluralism of values and authorities, and institutionalized individualism. On the cultural plane, it appears to favor forms of composite identity in which global and local traits mix, imposing a conflicting coexistence of several images of self ("cosmopolite identities" [see Beck, 2006]

As we know from our direct experience and not just through theoretical thinking, this modernity is characterized by a dimension of *global risks* (Beck, 2000): environmental crises; international terrorism; economic (but also health) threats of the planetary kind; new modes of social inequality, beginning with the increasing poverty of ever-vaster areas of the world; and interwoven with them, new forms of underemployment with devastating existential effects. In this scenario, the image of the future as controllable and governable time, in agreement with the first modernity's vision, is shrinking. Whereas the latter can be considered an expression of the Enlightenment view of overcoming the notion of limits—starting with those tied to knowledge—contemporary modernity forces us to face the impossibility of realizing any control (Leccardi, 1999). If the future seen by the first modernity was the open future, the future viewed by contemporary modernity is the *indeterminate* and *indeterminable future* governed by the interweaving of new risks and unforeseen possibilities.

This latter aspect has strategic importance in understanding the extent of the changes that have occurred in interpreting and experiencing the future. In this scenario, risk appears to be more the result of a loss of relationship between intention and result, between instrumental rationality and control, rather than (in the common scientific meaning) of relationship between an event and the probability that it will occur. Whereas in the first modernity the term *risk* was basically used to conceptualize a way of calculating unforeseen consequences—in essence, of "making the unpredictable predictable" by calculating probabilities—in contemporary modernity, thinking about risks requires conceptual tools of another type. In fact, these risks do not appear governable through methods of instrumental rationality; they are risks of global reach, and preventing them is arduous in the extreme.

The peculiar uncertainty that these risks generate is linked primarily to their *humanly produced* character, brought about by the growth in knowledge that characterizes our age: climatic mutations (think of the ozone hole), risks tied to nuclear weapons and power plants, and diseases like bovine spongiform encephalopathy ("mad cow disease") and severe, acute respiratory syndrome, or SARS. Therefore, in an era of global risks like ours, the enormous process (begun by the first modernity) of "colonizing the future" is interrupted. The future tends to escape our governing, with profound repercussions in the political and social spheres. The new reality generated by the spread of global risks transforms the future from the "promised land" to a scenario that is uncertain, if not openly menacing to collective and individual existence.

It is important to emphasize the close tie that exists between the spread of these particular types of global risks and a vision of the future. By their very nature, in fact, these risks are actually constructed and nourished by their relationship with the future, although they tell us nothing about what we should pursue in future. These risks do not speak to us of "the good" but concentrate exclusively on "the evils" the future can bring. So the idea of the future is simultaneously undefined and fraught with a diffuse sense of alarm together with a feeling of impotence.

New Forms of Conceptualizing Time

The scenarios of overwhelming risks we have mentioned—among other things, able to project themselves over long periods of time; the time gap between acts and their effects can, in the "global-risk society," be very long (Adam, 1998)—have fallout in ways of conceptualizing time that are worth dwelling on. If by temporal perspective we mean that perspective through which past, present, and future, memory, experience, and expectations are constantly and reciprocally related and coordinated, then in an age of diffused risks, the ability to live temporally passes through a crisis. A future horizon occupied by the risk dimension impedes, for example, the construction both of biographical narratives in which the dimension of continuity (each event is linked to another, and one can sensibly imagine influencing them) plays a strategic role and of an image of the present as a dimension that prepares the future.

This pulverization of the experience of time brings with it a special attention to the present, "the only dimension of time that is frequented without unease and on which attention dwells without difficulty" (Tabboni, 1986, p. 123). Once again, young people are a barometer especially sensitive to these transformations. As early as the 1980s, research into young people's time (Cavalli, 1985) revealed, for example, a shift from future to present, in particular the "extended present," as the area for potentially governing social and individual time.

The term *extended present* means the temporal area that borders on the present, a space that acquires new value with the growth of temporal acceleration, in turn favored by the velocity of technological times and the need for flexibility that is their corollary. According to Nowotny (1994), who delved into this concept, once the impractical category of future has been abolished, it becomes necessary to reformulate the concept of present, making it a central reference for contemporary temporal horizons. In this perspective, it is no longer the future but the extended present—that time span short enough not to escape the social and human domain but long enough to allow for some sort of projection further in time—that becomes the new time of action. In substance, in late-20th century time frames, the present looks like the only temporal dimension available for defining choices, an authentic existential horizon that, in a certain sense, *includes* and *replaces* future and past.

In this framework, we can clearly see an erosion in the idea of a project itself, defined as a form of selection, subjectively constructed, between the many "virtual futures" available, able to distill, from the fantasies and desires underlying them, pursuable aims having a clear temporal span.

But can one still speak of "biography" in the absence of a project? The first modernity delineated a scenario in which the two terms not only presupposed one another but the collective and the individual projects were two sides of the same coin. The aims of the collective project—freedom, democracy, equality, prosperity—appeared to be basic conditions for realizing the individual project. In turn, biographical narratives were structured around this coinciding. The second modernity tends to erase, along with temporal continuity, the idea of project and biography that the zenith of modernity constructed.

Making strides in this context is a tendency to experiment—not taken, however, as the customary reference to trial-and-error method aimed at finding the paths most suitable for reaching a given goal. The process is inverted. "We tend to go on trying different applications of the skills, talents and other resources which we have or hope to have, and try to find out which result brings more satisfaction" (Bauman & Tester, 2001, p. 90). This leads to an orientation on the basis of which "the secret of success is not to be unduly conservative, to refrain from habitualization to any particular bed, [to] be mobile and perpetually at hand" (Bauman & Tester, 2001, p. 90).

Changing Meanings of Youth

How these processes reflect on action models, lifestyles, and ways of defining identity can be easily intuited. In accord with the theme dealt with here, I would call attention in particular to the role that these changes play in reconsidering the youthful stage of life itself. By definition, in fact, this stage has a dual connection with time: on the one hand, it is considered a temporary condition, destined to disappear as time passes; on the other, as we have emphasized, young people are socially required to construct positive forms of relationships between their own time of life and social time. Until a few decades ago, for young men this took on substance in linear and easily recognizable biographical stages: first, preparation for work through education; then remunerated work, a central source of identity and undisputed sign of adulthood; and finally, retirement.

Today this biographical trajectory, able to guarantee a predictable path toward entry into adult life, is no longer the rule but the exception. For young people, the process of deinstitutionalizing the course of life, bringing with it the end of the concept of the "normal biography," leads to the disappearance of an aspect that was up to now determinant in concepts of the condition of youth: youth's identification with a set of steps, socially standardized, that progressively led to the adult world (Chisholm, Büchner, Krüger, & du Bois-Reymond, 1995; Chisholm, 1999; Coté, 2000; du Bois-Reymond, 1998; Furlong & Cartmel, 1997; Leccardi & Ruspini, 2006; Wallace & Kovatcheva, 1998; Wyn & White, 1997). These steps, habitually summarized under the term *transition*, identified the youth stage with a "crossing" guided by steps in status and guaranteed by the interweave between time of life and social time on the basis of an easily recognizable linear sequence. One became adult in the full sense once one had covered that route, which foresaw, in rapid succession, steps such as ending one's studies, joining the work world, leaving the parental home for independent living, creating one's own family nucleus, and having children (Buzzi, Cavalli, & de Lillo, 2002). Today, although these events are destined to happen sooner or later, their order and irreversibility seem to have been lost, along with the social framework that guaranteed their overall meaning.

Even more than from the sequentiality, linearity, and rapid succession of the single steps, this framework of meaning resulted from the *symbolic value* that these had as a whole in the life of a young individual. Through them, in fact, while confirming the "set-time" nature of the youthful stage of life, the two poles of autonomy (inner) and independence (social) could enter into a positive conjunction. In a word, youth conceived of as a transitional phase made it possible to think of the relationship between individual identity and social identity as of one between two dimensions not only complementary but also almost perfectly superimposed. Inner autonomy was achieved by the progressive passage to ever greater degrees of independence, made possible by the relationship with social institutions sufficiently credible and nonfragmented.

This scenario has now changed. Social institutions continue to pace the timing of the quotidian, but there has been a considerable weakening of their ability to guarantee a dimension fundamental to constructing individuality: the sense of biographical continuity. As a socially standardized trajectory toward adulthood slowly disappears, biographical continuity becomes the result of an individual ability to construct and reconstruct evernew frameworks of meaning for one's own decisions despite the present-based time frame.

As a consequence, the obligation to individualize biographies—searching for biographical solutions better suited to resolving the moment's systemic contradictions—characterizes the phase of history in which we live (Beck & Beck-Gernsheim, 2003). This implies a new emphasis on self-determination, autonomy, and choice (without, obviously, erasing the ruts made by differences in class, ethnic group, and on a perhaps less apparent but no less powerful plane, gender). For young people, all of this translates into conquering new areas of freedom and experimentation but also into a loss of the taken-for-granted character of a positive relationship with social time frames.

Although it is true that the lengthening of the youth stage is certainly the most obvious aspect nowadays, the decisive transformation consists nevertheless of the loss of an ability to anchor the experiences that young people go through to the world of social and political institutions. The crisis of the future, and of the project, that we have looked at is a direct expression of this difficulty.

Redefining the Future: Youthful Biographical Constructions in a Time of Uncertainty

For young people, at the core of this crisis is the disconnection between life trajectories, social roles, and ties to the universe of institutions able to give a stable shape to identity. Thus, for example, one can enter the job market, leave shortly afterward, and then reenter it without being able to identify in these exits and entrances a progression toward the assumption of adult roles. Or university studies can be concluded without having the acquisition of degree credentials represent a true milestone on the biographical plane, an empowerment able to open the way to new existential situations: not only to a career but also, for example, in Mediterranean Europe, to opting to live alone or with a partner or to creating one's own family. In a word, existential autonomy is increasingly disassociated from the acquisition of social and financial independence.

However, it is essential not to limit thinking solely to the aspects of loss: of fewer chances to act that are associated with the second modernity's processes of redefining time. In fact, there is also another side to these self-same processes, a visible one that deserves equal attention. On it are drawn the strategies that people construct to deal with these transformations and, where possible, control them. As also shown by the aforementioned recent research into the changes in how young people relate to time (Crespi, 2005), the outcome of these important processes of restructuring the relationship between young people, biographical time, and social time does not boil down to making the immediate present absolute, to glorifying the here and now. Identities are not based solely on the present. Although this option does transpire from a number of interviews, it does not exclude other responses. Some young people seem, for example, to be involved in a search for new modes of relating the process of personal production and creation (in any case associated with the future) to the specific conditions of uncertainty in which the future is now experienced (Leccardi, 2005b).

The future is, therefore, viewed in relation to potential openings—more than ever today, the future is an area of possible becoming—and at the same time to an indeterminateness increasingly felt as insecurity. In other words, within the virtuality that, by definition, characterizes the future is delineated a peculiar interweaving between the "anarchization" of the future, to use Grosz's expression (1999), and hesitation, anxiety, and the desire, more or less unconscious, to substitute dream for project. Faced with the future's increasingly ambivalent traits, fundamental is a person's ability to work out cognitive strategies able to guarantee control over time of life despite the increase in contingency.

In recent research conducted on French and Spanish young people from which a similar biographical orientation emerged, this was effectively defined as an *indetermination strategy* (Lasen, 2001). This term is meant to underscore the growing capacity of young people with greater reflexive resources to read the uncertainty of the future as a multiplication of virtual possibilities and the unpredictability associated with it as added potential instead of a limit to action. In other words, faced with a future less and less traceable to the present through an ideal line uniting them and reciprocally heightening their meaning, a number of young people—perhaps not the majority, but certainly culturally mobile—work out responses able to neutralize a paralyzing fear of the future.

Likewise, some of the young people we interviewed (young men and young women to the same extent) clearly expressed a tendency to be open in a positive way to the unexpected, reckoning in advance with the possibility of sudden changes in course, of having to construct responses "in real time" as occasions present themselves. The speed training that social rhythms impose is, in this case, exploited for the best: being quick becomes a must, enables one, in a positive way, to reap opportunities, to begin experimentation that can have a positive effect on time of life as a whole.

For these young people, the uncertainty of the future, therefore, means a willingness to encounter the accidental, the fortuitous: an opportunity that many of our interviewees seem to like. Here control over biographical time is not identified with the ability to go ahead with specific projects, neutralizing any unexpected things encountered along the way. Rather, control is equivalent to the will to reach the general goals one has set: most young people, while lacking life projects proper, have one or more broad goals located in the future in regard to work or private life—in other words, "taking care of oneself" Foucault-like (1987). The innovative aspect of this new biographical construction—at whose center is a tending toward a "future without project" but not without control—is the ability to accept the fragmentation and uncertainty of what surrounds us as an irreversible reality to be transformed into resources by constantly exercising awareness and reflexivity.

It should immediately be stressed that the young people expressing this temporal strategy seem to be especially rich in cultural, social, and economic resources. If today's elite is distinguishable for its ability to make good use, for power purposes, of speed and mobility, these young people appear to be part of its wake. On the other hand, those with meager social and cultural resources seem above all to suffer from the loss of the first modernity's progressive future and traditional project creating. For these young people, the future, outside of control, can only be annulled or cancelled out to make room for an unappealing present. In their case (as well-described by Castel, 2002, reflecting on contemporary individualism), we are faced with a form of individualism by default: here individuals do not possess the supports needed to construct their own autonomy and are flattened into an identity lacking temporal consistency. Social speed-up thus patently becomes a source of social exclusion translating into suffered stasis.

In response to highly insecure and risky social conditions, most young people—men and women—take refuge mainly in short- and very-short-term projects, taking the extended present as the temporal area of reference. They react to the short time frames of acceleration society with a sui generis type of project creation that is expressed in minimal time spans and, also because of this, appears malleable. In some cases, it appears to be essentially configured as a reaction to the unease that the idea of the future itself evokes; in others, it assumes the characteristic of projects imprinted with concreteness—mostly tied to successfully finishing activities already commenced—able to respond both to the need to master biographical time in a fast-paced and uncertain environment and to social pressure for short-term results. In this latter case, "short project" typology looks like a sort of middle road between the special ability to manage complexity proper to the first kind of biographical orientation considered (able to relate to the future without formulating projects) and the exclusive reference to the present of those unable to construct reactions adequate to the growing uncertainty of the future.

In fact, concentrating on a temporally limited area makes it possible to construct an experience of time as a unified and continuous field that is subjectively controllable; in turn, dominion over times of life is striven for not by working out goals distant in time (an unrealistic aim in an age of uncertainty) but by engaging in them here and now. This middle-road strategy looks especially attractive because whereas it does not entirely impede a projection into the future through the project, it is in tune with the flexible orientation made necessary by an era in which the processes of change are rapid and often unpredictable.

Conclusion

At a time when the medium- to long-term future cannot be discussed without creating unease or actual dread, a method of action based on a case-by-case assessment—on "when doors open for me, I try not to shut them" or on reaping opportunity as soon as it appears—can be a rational strategy for transforming unpredictability into opportunity, the opacity of the future into a chance for the present. For being disposed to becoming.

Although in this scenario the delayed gratification mechanism confirms its inadequacy as a reference standard for social action, a growing number of young people nonetheless appear able to replace it with models of action built around new forms of temporal discipline, of planning and control attentive to everyday time, for example, for brief and fixed-term but intense periods.

In a historic period of future crisis—and of upheaval in conceiving of youth as a transition to adulthood—there is appearing a new way to regard time. At its heart is the need to be at ease about the speed of events, to control change by equipping oneself for prompt action instead of "letting things happen," to overcome a diffuse feeling of insecurity. Even if the time being lived in is terribly uncertain, what appears to be important is above all staying on course, not losing one's inner direction. Control over time is no longer exercised by means of life plans as traditionally understood (goals related to time of life; the ability to pace, on this basis, short, medium, and long times; and the ability to accept current frustration with the view of achieving future goals). Rather, it seems to result from the ability to keep open the horizon of the possible, creating the conditions for revising the priority of action in the light of arriving changes.

In this scenario, it is not only the meaning of time and of the future, in particular, that is transformed. There is also consolidation of a different conception of action and strategy, a construction that requires individuals to think of themselves as autonomous centers; to take permanent responsibility for themselves; and to feel ever ready for battle, ready to transform, in real time, potential constraints into as many resources. A new figure—that of the permanently active individual, able to work out a personal biography in an activist way, always ready to explore the new frontiers that accelerated society opens—is particularly in tune with this redefinition of the future.

Note

1. The research, financed jointly by the Italian Ministry of Education and individual universities, involved various academic institutions: in the north, the University of Milan-Bicocca and the University of Pavia; in central Italy, the universities of Florence and of Perugia; and on the islands, the University of Cagliari (Sardinia).

Whereas the universities at Milan-Bicocca, Pavia, and Perugia took into consideration the relationship between young people, biographical time, and daily time, those of Cagliari and Florence restricted themselves to looking at how daily time was used and experienced. The principal instrument of the inquiry was in-depth interviews. The University of Perugia also made use of focus groups. The universities at Cagliari and Florence used diaries as well as the interviews (and avoided time budgets, considered unsuitable for the study of subjective representations connected to the use of daily time). The interviews, performed in 2002 in the cities listed above, involved 200 young people of both sexes between the ages of 18 and 29 (students, manual and non-manual laborers, young people who study and work, and unemployed youth and dropouts).

References

Adam, B. (1998). *Timescapes of modernity: The environment and invisible hazards*. London: Routledge.

Bauman, Z. (1995). *Life in fragments: Essays in postmodern morality*. Oxford, U.K.: Blackwell.

Bauman, Z. (2000). *Liquid modernity*. Cambridge, U.K.: Polity Press.

Bauman, Z., & Tester, K. (2001). *Conversations with Zygmunt Bauman*. Cambridge, U.K.: Polity Press.

Beck, U. (1999). *World risk society*. London: Sage.

Beck, U. (2000). Risk society revisited: Theory, politics and research programmes. In B. Adam, U. Beck, & J. van Loon (Eds.), *The risk society and beyond: Critical issues for social theory* (pp. 211–229). London: Sage.

Beck, U. (2006). *Cosmopolitan vision*. Cambridge, U.K.: Polity Press.

Beck, U., & Beck-Gernsheim, E. (2003). *Individualization: Institutionalized individualism and its social and political consequences*. London: Sage.

Buzzi, C., Cavalli, A., & de Lillo, A. (Eds.) (2002). *Giovani del nuovo secolo* [Youth in the new century]. Bologna: Il Mulino.

Castel, R. (2002). *From manual workers to wage laborers: Transformation of the social question*. Somerset, NJ: Transaction.

Cavalli, A. (1980). La gioventù: Condizione o processo? [Youth: A condition or a process?]. *Rassegna Italiana di Sociologia, 4*, 519–531.

Cavalli, A. (Ed.) (1985). *Il tempo dei giovani* [Youth and time]. Bologna: Il Mulino.

Chisholm, L. (1999). From systems to networks: The reconstruction of youth transitions in Europe. In W. Heinz (Ed.), *From education to work: Cross-national perspectives* (pp. 298–318). Cambridge, U.K.: Cambridge University Press.

Chisholm, L., Büchner, P., Krüger H.-H., & du Bois-Reymond, M. (Eds.) (1995). *Growing up in Europe: Contemporary horizons in childhood and youth studies*. Berlin: Gruyter.

Coté, J. (2000). *Arrested adulthood: The changing nature of maturity and identity*. New York: New York University Press.

Crespi, F. (Ed.) (2005). *Tempo vola: L'esperienza del tempo nella società contemporanea* [Time flies: Time experience in contemporary society]. Bologna: Il Mulino.

du Bois-Reymond, M. (1998). "I don't want to commit myself yet": Young people's life concepts. *Journal of Youth Studies, 1(1)*, 63–79.

Foucault, M. (1987). The ethic of care for the self as a practice of freedom: An interview. *Philosophy and Social Criticism, 12(2/3)*, 112–131.

Furlong, A., & Cartmel, F. (1997). *Young people and social change: Individualization and risk in late modernity*. Buckingham, U.K.: Open University Press.

Grosz, E. (1999). Thinking the new: Of futures yet unthought. In *Becomings: Explorations in time, memory and futures* (pp. 11–28). Ithaca, NY: Cornell University Press.

Lasen, A. (2001). *Le temps des jeunes: Rythmes, durée et virtualités* [Time and youth: Rhythms, duration and virtualities]. Paris: L'Harmattan.

Leccardi, C. (Ed.) (1999). *Limiti della modernità: Trasformazioni del mondo e della conoscenza* [Limits of modernity: Transformations of the world and of knowledge]. Rome: Carocci.

Leccardi, C. (2005a). Facing uncertainty: Temporality and biographies in the new century. *Young: Nordic Journal of Youth Research, 13*(2), 123–146.

Leccardi, C. (2005b). I tempi di vita tra accelerazione e lentezza [Times of life between acceleration and slowness]. In F. Crespi (Ed.), *Tempo vola: L'esperienza del tempo nella società contemporanea* [Time flies: Time experience in contemporary society] (pp. 49–85). Bologna: Il Mulino.

Leccardi, C., & Ruspini, E. (Eds.) (2006). *A new youth? Young people, generations and family life.* Aldershot, U.K.: Ashgate.

Nowotny, H. (1994). *Time: The modern and postmodern experience.* Cambridge, U.K.: Polity Press.

Rampazi, M. (1985). Il tempo biografico [Biographical time]. In A. Cavalli (Ed.), *Il tempo dei giovani* [Youth and time] (pp. 149–263). Bologna: Il Mulino.

Rosa, H. (2003). Social acceleration: Ethical and political consequences of a desynchronized high-speed society. *Constellations, 10*(1), 3–33.

Tabboni, S. (1986). Le radici quotidiane della rappresentazione del tempo storico [The representation of historical time and its quotidian roots]. In M. C. Belloni (Ed.), *L'aporia del tempo* [The aporia of time] (pp. 121–133). Milan: Angeli.

Tocqueville, A. de (1835–1840/1966). *Democracy in America.* New York: Harper.

Wallace, C., & Kovatcheva, S. (1998). *Youth in society: The construction and deconstruction of youth in East and West Europe.* Houndmills-Basingstoke, U.K.: Palgrave.

Wyn, J., & White, R. (1997). *Rethinking youth.* London: Sage.

CARMEN LECCARDI *is full professor of cultural sociology at the University of Milano-Bicocca, Italy. Her main research interests relate to youth cultures, time, and gender issues.*

NEW DIRECTIONS FOR CHILD AND ADOLESCENT DEVELOPMENT • DOI: 10.1002/cad

5

This chapter presents an overview of studies investigating the role of the family while children cope with problems in their transitions to the labor market. Attention is paid to different support systems in a variety of European countries, depending on different state welfare models.

Social Change, Family Support, and Young Adults in Europe

Andrew Biggart, Siyka Kovacheva

Over the past few decades, the nature of transitions to adulthood has changed radically across Europe. Young adult transitions have become more individualized, complex, and prolonged (see Chapter 7), and many young people in Europe face difficulties in establishing their economic independence. As a result, they are increasingly dependent or semidependent on their families for a protracted time, and the relationships between young adults and their families are becoming an increasingly salient topic for both policy and research.

Patterns of family dependency differ significantly across European national contexts, and although this can be partly explained by different cultural traditions, the ways in which resources and opportunities are governed through institutional factors such as the market, the state, and the family are also key aspects in explaining these diverse patterns. In this chapter, we aim to explore, within the context of modern socioeconomic change and the protraction of young people's transitions to adulthood, the changing nature of the relationships between young people and their parents. We begin by assessing recent European literature on young people's transitions to adulthood before going on to examine conceptual issues surrounding family support. Finally, we draw on research provided by one of the few European comparative studies in this area, the Families and Transitions in Europe (FATE) project. In this project, the investigators aimed to explore significant implications of the changing nature of young people's transitions to adulthood, for both young people and their parents; it was conducted

NEW DIRECTIONS FOR CHILD AND ADOLESCENT DEVELOPMENT, no. 113, Fall 2006 © Wiley Periodicals, Inc.
Published online in Wiley InterScience (www.interscience.wiley.com) • DOI: 10.1002/cad.168

49

across a range of European contexts, covering the United Kingdom, Germany (East and West), Denmark, Netherlands, Bulgaria, Italy, Portugal, and Spain. We draw on qualitative data from this project to highlight key differences across the main welfare models in Europe and examine the specific issues facing one of the former socialist states, Bulgaria.

Family and the Transition to Adulthood in Europe

Modern socioeconomic change is affecting young adults and their families in complex and diverse ways, and although there are a number of general trends across Europe, the nature of these changes is by no means homogenous. Only recently has there been a renewed focus on the family as an important institution; before this, it had become relatively neglected by most European academic and policy discourses. Some would suggest that it was perceived as an out-of-date institution, a residue of traditional societies that predates the formation of the welfare state (Sgritta, 2001). European comparative studies that have focused on the issue of the family have tended to be in relation to young children, in particular the difficulties women face in reconciling work and family life (Drew, Emerek, & Mahon, 1998); differences in family policy (Hantrais, 2004); or the changing nature of family forms with increasing rates of divorce, cohabitation, and single parents (Kaufmann, Knijsten, Schulze, & Strohmeier, 2002).

The renewed academic and policy interest in the family as an important social actor in relation to young adults' transitions appears to stem from a number of sources. First, major policy concerns have arisen over the impact of declining fertility rates; in most European countries, these have now fallen well below replacement rates. And whereas there has been a strong tradition of examining family characteristics as a means of explaining persistent inequalities in educational and occupational destinations (Couch, 1999; Shavit & Blossfeld, 1993), only recently have the different cultural expectations of the family in supporting dependent young adults increasingly been recognized.

One of the most commonly used comparative indicators of young adults' economic independence is the age at which they leave the parental home, and the earlier general trend in Europe from the 1960s to 1980s toward leaving the home earlier has now reversed (Iacovou, 2001; Iacovou & Berthoud, 2001; Chisholm & Kovacheva, 2002). Although a deferred exit from the parental home is common across Europe, the division between the north and south is considerable. For example, at age 23, those in the south of Europe are three times more likely than their northern European counterparts to be still living in the parental home (Iacovou & Berthoud, 2001). Whereas all of southern Europe is characterized by a late departure from the parental home, the Italian context is most extreme: it is not until the age of 30, in the case of men, and 27 in the case of women, when half of young people have departed the parental home (Iacovou, 2001). Although the differences in leaving the parental home are well documented, we know less about the determinants of leaving home. Home leaving is only one indicator of adulthood, and young people may live in a variety of states of dependency: they may be economically independent and remain at home, leave home to study but be financially dependent on their parents, and live in a variety of states in between. Iacovou (2001) shows how young people from Scandinavia are much more likely to leave home as singles whereas in southern Europe young people most often leave to form a partnership. Jones (2005), however, warns of how aggregate statistics on leaving the parental home may distort the complexity of the process of home leaving. In northern Europe, young people may leave home much earlier for reasons other than marriage, only to return at a later stage; therefore, this calls into question the significance of home leaving as an indicator of economic independence.

Clearly another important dimension in achieving independence is young people's access to stable paid employment, and European labor markets have shown little sign of convergence, with significant variation in the labor market opportunities for the young (European Commission, 2003). Previous research has also highlighted cross-national variation in the types of linkages between education and employment (Müller & Shavit, 1997; Müller & Gangl, 2003). Although such comparative analyses of young adults' transitions to the labor market have focused on the different institutional linkages, the recent inclusion of southern European contexts into existing theoretical frameworks has proved difficult. It is suggested that the extensive family support in southern Europe enables young people to wait until they can find employment at an appropriate level (Gangl, 2001). Sgritta (1999), on the other hand, argues how in the Italian case, young people's decisions are more than simply a response to their objective conditions. Instead, he highlights a cultural shift in young people's attitudes to independence whereby remaining in the family home has become an attractive choice.

In considering the role of the family in young people's transition to adulthood, we must also consider the changing nature of families themselves. European family studies describe families as being challenged by increased responsibility and that middle-aged parents often have responsibilities to provide support both for their parents and their dependent children (Attias-Donfut & Wolff, 2000). This is perhaps at a time when the family itself, at least in its traditional nuclear form, is increasingly unstable.

Despite the prolonged dependency of young adults and the growing recognition of the importance of relationships within the family and its resources for young adults' transitions, European comparative research within this area remains limited (Dey & Morris, 1999). However, assumptions surrounding parental support for young people in European countries are changing significantly, and although the family is increasingly used as a means to explain European differences, conceptually it has tended to remain largely concealed within a black box (Biggart & Walther, 2005).

New Directions for Child and Adolescent Development • DOI: 10.1002/cad

Conceptualizing Family Support for Young Adults

Before considering some of the central concepts that surround family or parental support in a European comparative context, we should perhaps acknowledge that definitions surrounding the concepts of youth, adulthood, and the family are themselves problematic. Although we have suggested above that social change may be weakening the family as an institution, it is not our intention here to go into a detailed discussion of trying to define a European family model. There is much disagreement over definitions of the family in contemporary Europe (for a discussion, see Cheal, 1999), but few would deny that the recognized boundaries of families have become more fluid and diversified (Hantrais, 2004). In a similar vein, the traditional objective markers between youth and adulthood have become increasingly blurred, and one distinction that may be made is in young people's *dependency*, which can be defined as a socioeconomic concept, and *autonomy* as a concept that relates to identity processes (van de Velde, 2001; Biggart & Walther, 2005).

Another distinction that can be drawn is in the cultural or subjective expectations about patterns of family life in Europe. The expected role of the family changes according to family models, welfare regime, and in line with cultural norms and models of residence peculiar to each country. We can distinguish different models of social regulation, which are constituted by the interrelationship between responsibilities attributed to the welfare state and those that are attributed to the family (Gallie & Paugam, 2000).

In the Scandinavian countries, with a universalistic welfare regime, the role of the family in supporting young adults is more likely to be a marginal one. The assumption in these countries is that society has a collective responsibility for its members and that each individual member has the right to be protected by the welfare state irrespective of the situation of his or her family. Accordingly, these countries have high proportions of young people receiving social transfers from the government.

In the southern European countries, there is a strong correspondence between the subprotective welfare regime and the extended-dependence model. The underlying assumption of this model of social regulation is that the family will provide the support that the welfare regime does not. Because protection offered by the subprotective regime is limited, correspondingly, the role of the family in the support of its members is stronger.

In mid-European countries such as the Netherlands, Belgium, Ireland, Germany, France, and the United Kingdom, responsibility for providing support for young people is divided between the state and the family. In this sense, welfare states may provide for the minimum needs of the young person, or a social safety net, while the family takes responsibility for the broader protection of living standards. The assumption in this model of social regulation is that support provided by the family is not a responsibility that the family would normally be expected to assume.

NEW DIRECTIONS FOR CHILD AND ADOLESCENT DEVELOPMENT • DOI: 10.1002/cad

Finally, there are the European postsocialist states, which are diverging in different ways from the centralized state system of extensive state support for young adults' transitions under the former communist regime. Here the picture is much more fluid, and these countries are diverging in different ways; for example, Bulgaria is becoming more closely aligned with the southern European model, with limited welfare support, whereas Slovenia is building on its previous universal policies and in some respects resembles the universalistic regimes of the Scandinavian countries.

Although different cultural and institutional models may influence young adults transitions and the expectations and the necessity of family support across European national contexts, conceptualizing the forms of support young adults may receive during their transition to adulthood is particularly difficult because of the diversity in the nature and extent of family support a young person can expect to receive. Here the potential resources of the family are clearly crucial; however, young people's access to available resources not only may be dependent on need but may have to be negotiated within the family. Parents may withhold support as a means of fostering independence, or alternatively, young people may reject support so as to demonstrate autonomy (Holdsworth & Morgan, 2005).

The sociological concept of different "capitals" also provides a possibility to understand and conceptualize many aspects of social integration in the modern world. It was Bourdieu and Passeron (1977) who first drew attention to the sociological potential of the different forms of capital: they differentiate between economic, cultural, and social capital. Because the structural conditions under which young adults make their transitions across Europe differ, Bourdieu and Passeron's accounts of the interplay between structure and agency offer the potential to examine how different family practices serve to produce different outcomes.

The economic capital of the family is clearly central to the provision of material support to dependent or semidependent young adults. Cultural capital, on the other hand, is less easily defined and remains a vague concept. It is seen to stem mainly from socialization within the family, and it may be useful in understanding the source of young people's beliefs or why parents support their adult children for some things and not others (Jones, 2005).

In recent years, the concept of social capital has become particularly fashionable, although it remains a contested and differentiated concept within the social sciences. The way the concept is often operationalized through the use of quantitative indicators focuses more on social capital as a structural feature of communities and regions and much less on the role of the family in the development of social capital. However, the recent literature reviews on social capital (Edwards, Franklin, & Holland, 2003; Edwards, 2004; Mihailova, 2004) suggest that large-scale value surveys neglect subtler microprocesses such as parenting styles, communications, investment in time, and mutual expectations through which families generate social capital. Social capital can also serve as a useful heuristic device for exploring processes and practices that are related to the acquisition of other forms of capital (Ball, 2003; Morrow, 1999).

Young Adults, the Family, and the European Welfare State

One of the aims of the FATE project was to begin to try to understand how the different institutional arrangements that exist across the different welfare models in Europe interact to produce different subjective responses both in the decisions of young adults and the respective parenting practices in the contemporary context. Around 45 young adults were interviewed about one year after leaving a range of levels of postcompulsory education in each national context and, where possible, interviews were also conducted with one or both parents. We draw on this material to highlight some of the different ways that subjective responses are influenced by different expectations of family support across three welfare contexts, before going on to consider the specific case of one of the former socialist states, Bulgaria.

Denmark is representative of the universalistic welfare regime, and social change has affected Danish society in many ways. It is characterized by high levels of nonconventional family forms, high rates of divorce, and reconstituted families. Young adults' transitions have become prolonged compared with those of the previous generation, but labor market opportunities for the young remain comparatively favorable.

Family obligations are confined to those younger than 18 years, and parents are therefore largely freed from supporting their adult children economically. From the age of 18, state welfare provides generous educational allowances, and although these may not be sufficient for total independence, most young people combine them with part-time work and become financially independent from their families at an early stage. Most of our respondents had left the parental home before age 20.

With comparatively favorable labor market conditions, one might expect young adults' transitions through education to the labor market to remain relatively smooth, following a linear path; however, this frequently proved not to be the case. Absent constraint by the material resources of the family and with an open and flexible education system, numerous possibilities arise. Because young adults are constrained only by their own personal resources and assumptions about what is desirable and possible, they often used this space that extensive state support provides as a period of self-actualization and reflection. Decisions over the final direction of educational and occupational pathways were commonly found to be delayed: young people took time out to travel, to establish a family, or just to pursue some other personal goal.

For the parents, the familial role mainly appeared to be about preparing young people with the competencies to cope with independent life, equipping them with decision-making skills and the ability to manage their own resources. Some parents intentionally withheld economic support from the moment their child turned 18 as a means of fostering independence. Even among the more affluent families, the ability to influence transitions beyond the transmission of emotional and cultural capital was limited and appeared to run contrary to parental assumptions. And whereas mobilizing the economic and social capital of the family may run contrary to parental practices and policy assumptions, among those from less affluent backgrounds, it was the cultural capital of the family that appeared to set particular boundaries that could be difficult to overcome.

> I could not see it before I became 26 to 27 years old; I could not imagine that this was what I wanted. And I didn't dare to go to a university because no one in my family has ever completed more than compulsory school. . . . it's unspoken that at least we don't do that kind of thing, or . . . the universities are for "the nice and well-born" and if so, you are snobbish and that kind of stuff. . . . to liberate myself from this attitude would mean that I would be totally alienated in relation to my family. It took me many years to dare to do that. [Majken, 32-year-old female, psychology graduate]

In contrast to the Danish case, the southern European contexts and, in particular, Italy, are very different. Here the family retains a much more traditional role, both in form and in family obligations, where with minimal state support, young adults' transitional routes were often highly dependent on the resources of the family. Transitions were a family project, rather than an individual one, and were more dependent on the economic, social, and cultural capital of the family. With a high level of youth unemployment and a labor market that favors and protects men, young adults have few opportunities to enter the formal labor market, and extended education, supported through familial resources becomes a crucial resource in accessing stable employment.

Although we may expect the availability of the economic capital of the family to have a major influence on decisions to pursue extended education, and undoubtedly this plays a major role, less affluent parents also displayed an acute awareness of the importance of qualifications in the modern labor market and often made considerable personal sacrifices to promote the education of their offspring.

The availability of family resources, however, appeared to influence educational pathways in several respects. Young adults from higher socioeconomic backgrounds tended to enjoy unlimited family support in every respect of their lives: a comfortable existence within the family home, their own car, and the latest mobile phone. Among less affluent families, although parents were willing to assist in supporting decisions to remain in education, their attitude was more ambivalent, and when the motivation to continue in education broke down or educational grades were not achieved, parental financial support could be withdrawn, giving young adults little recourse but to enter unstable and low-paid segments of the labor market.

NEW DIRECTIONS FOR CHILD AND ADOLESCENT DEVELOPMENT • DOI: 10.1002/cad

On making transitions to the labor market, those of all educational levels expect an extended period of unemployment to be normal, and most families were happy to continue to support their offspring in the waiting game until an appropriate job arose. This was either fully supported by the family or supplemented through temporary forms of employment, while the family itself and its wider social network still proved to be an important resource in assisting young people's entry into the labor market.

Despite the high levels of economic dependency on the family, parents gave young people a high level of autonomy within the parental home and in the choices they make over their transitions, and leaving the familial home was still largely predicated on the achievement of full economic independence and in the event of marriage. Most parents appear to have adapted to this new condition of youth. They say their generation was forced to leave the parental home because of a lack of autonomy and a desire to escape the restrictions imposed by their parents. Aware of the difficulties young adults have in securing their own independence in the contemporary context, they provided them with a largely unrestricted lifestyle within the parental home.

"These young people feel the need for the family because they're well off. . . . I think it's also very convenient for them because they don't have the problem of having to get married to get their freedom, even sexual or otherwise. . . . They're free to do at home whatever they want, but all told, they don't want to take responsibility, . . . and they avoid having to adjust to living with someone else" (47-year-old housewife, mother of Walther).

The United Kingdom, representing the liberal-minimal region, takes a moderate position somewhere in between the extremes of Denmark and Italy. Here, although there was a strong tradition of early school leaving and early economic independence from the family achieved through paid employment, occupational restructuring from the mid-1970s has led to a situation where good educational credentials are increasingly necessary. In the past, generous state support had been provided on a means-tested basis to a generally affluent minority pursuing higher education, and for the majority who entered the labor market at an early stage, independent housing and welfare support were available from the age of 16. However, with increasing educational expansion and a decline in labor market opportunities for the less qualified, the level of state support has been significantly curtailed. Except in cases of extreme hardship, benefit entitlements for young adults have been removed and grants for higher education replaced by a system of student loans and the responsibility for support increasingly placed on the individual and his or her family. In this context of change, family support to young adults is not seen as self-evident because it is not a traditionally expected state of affairs. Although among the most affluent parents, supporting the maintenance costs of young adults pursuing higher education tends to be perceived as natural, having received similar family support themselves, among those with more limited resources, extended economic dependency is not expected.

"I think it's ridiculous that nowadays there's been such a change and students are expected to pay so much. . . . it's ridiculous. I really don't think it's fair. . . . you can't expect a parent not to pay, and yet—they end up having to do without so that their children can have, you know—I just don't think its right" (Heather, 22-year-old woman, optometry graduate).

Because transitions through extended educational pathways are completed comparatively swiftly, with a comparatively short duration of study, unlike their counterparts in Denmark, the separation of education-to-work transitions from the broader transition to adulthood is less evident. And whereas some young people left home at an early stage to go away to study, they often returned on the completion of studies. As in the case of southern Europe, transitions out of the family home tend to continue to follow a more linear path but, in contrast, one that usually was achieved on the attainment of full economic independence, rather than marriage.

In the United Kingdom, at least in recent years, the labor market is relatively favorable, and although many young people after completing their education continue to follow smooth transitions into the labor market, others find themselves constrained by local opportunity structures. With limited state support and low expectations of family support, combined with a weakly regulated labor market, when young adults experience difficulties, they are often quick to downgrade their aspirations and to accept the next best available thing in order to achieve their financial independence. In this respect, we do not observe the same delaying strategies among young adults from the United Kingdom that were evident in other contexts, with neither the state nor the family providing a buffer at labor market entry.

Whereas rapid and profound social change has greatly affected young adults and their families in northern, western, and southern Europe, those European countries that are making the transition from centrally planned socialist states to market economies face their own set of issues. The FATE project included Bulgaria, one of the poorer of the former Soviet states, which provided an opportunity to examine the contemporary situation of youth and adulthood in a society that is undergoing profound cultural and socioeconomic change.

Under the former communist system, youth had been the main beneficiary of the welfare policy of the one-party regime, and young people's transitions to adulthood were strongly structured by the state education system and the centrally planned economy. There were clear-cut routes from school to work, which were assisted by the system of state allocation of graduates into jobs (Wallace & Kovatcheva, 1998).

Although family support for the younger generation had also been strong during communism, under the conditions of postcommunism, it has become an increasingly crucial resource as the previous clear-cut routes into employment collapsed and youth faced growing insecurity in their transitions (Mitev, 2005). The prolonged and increasingly insecure youth transitions have rendered new importance to family support (Alber & Fahey, 2004; Ule & Rener, 1998). In Bulgaria, it was the accepted norm for parents to provide as much support as they could to their adult children, with a perception among many parents that this was now essential because the institutions of the state seemed to be falling apart: "There is so much unemployment now. If the family cannot find a job for the young person, he is lost" (42-year-old hairdresser, mother of Geno).

Social contacts were perceived to have also grown in importance since the collapse of the communist system, and both parents and young people considered that to get a well-paid job, "connections" were crucial: "Education, skills, personal qualities have no value on our market; only connections matter" (Stoyan, 19-year-old male high school graduate).

As in the case of southern Europe, it is the accepted norm for Bulgarian families to provide support for their children. However, it was difficult to discern a dominant parenting style in our case study. Three different types of familial responses appeared to be emerging. The first type of family was characterized by a highly democratic style of parenting where young people's transitional decisions were taken among the whole family, and it was not just the parents who provided support: siblings also often played a key role both financially and emotionally, to a much greater extent than we witnessed in any other of the national contexts.

Parents perceived themselves as friends of their children, not as mentors or guardians. And whereas parents would do what they could to support their children financially and emotionally within their own often-limited means, it was often siblings who had successfully obtained a well-paid job who would support other siblings' transitions, which often included emigration to the West. In these families, young people were encouraged by their parents to make their own decisions but within the context of the whole family, including grandparents: "We advise her but do not direct her. We cannot make decisions instead of her. . . . We discuss everything together, and then she does what she decides herself" (47-year-old laboratory assistant, mother of Daniela).

Other Bulgarian families provided support in a different way: they tried to take control of all aspects of their children's lives, from educational and work decisions to their friendship networks, in an attempt to protect them and achieve what they consider they were denied under communism: "It is the parents who can direct their children in their transitions. It is the parents who should lead the children in their studies. It is the parents who can find them a proper job" (60-year-old retired school teacher, father of Milena).

Although parents often took extreme levels of control over their children's decisions, they also went to extreme lengths to compensate for the lack of institutional support. Many parents made major sacrifices in order to support their adult children, limiting their own consumption, selling property, or taking additional jobs and working long hours.

The final attitude that was observed among our Bulgarian families was what could be described as a strategy of noninterference. The parents seemed either unwilling or unable to mobilize what social capital they had. Many felt helpless: because circumstances had changed so much from their own experience, they felt they could not offer points of reference for their children's transitions and that it is unjust that the state neglects its responsibilities to the young. Their former networks and connections had often dissipated or become dysfunctional with economic restructuring, and many families felt that they lacked sufficient resources—educational, financial, and social—to influence young people's decisions and instead simply left young people to their own devices.

Conclusion

Across Europe, rapid socioeconomic change over the past few decades has radically altered the nature of young people's transitions to fully independent adulthood. A process of social change in most national contexts has been accompanied by either a direct or implicit reduction in the level of state provision for young adults in transition, and therefore, strong family support has become increasingly salient.

Although there has been a general lack of comparative European research into the implications for young people and their families of extended dependency, the FATE project has given some useful insights into the way in which the interrelationship between welfare regimes and the different expectations that surround family support serve to produce different responses among young adults and their parents. The study provides a rich body of evidence that young adults and their families, where state support is absent, try to compensate for this lack of support by mobilizing their economic, cultural, and social capital, albeit in a way that may serve to reproduce rather than alleviate existing inequalities. However, the research provides only a limited snapshot at a specific point in time, and it would require in-depth longitudinal research to completely understand the complexities of the process and the full implications for long-term outcomes.

References

Alber, J., & Fahey, T. (2004). *Perceptions of living conditions in an enlarged Europe*. Dublin: European Foundation for the Improvement of Living and Working Conditions.

Attias-Donfut, C., & Wolff, F.-C. (2000). The redistributive effects of generational transfers. In S. Arber & C. Attias-Donfut (Eds.), *The myth of generational conflict: The family and state in ageing societies* (pp. 22–46). London: Routledge.

Ball, S. (2003). *Class strategies and the education market: The middle classes and social advantages*. London: Routledge-Falmer.

Biggart, A., & Walther, A. (2005). Young adults' yo-yo transitions: Struggling for support between family and state in comparative perspective. In C. Leccardi & E. Ruspini (Eds.), *A new youth? Young people, generations and family life* (pp. 41–62). Aldershot, U.K.: Ashgate.

Bourdieu, P., & Passeron J. (1977). *Reproduction in education, society and culture*. London: Sage.

Cheal, D. (1999). The one and the many: Modernity and postmodernity. In G. Allan (Ed.), *The sociology of the family: A reader* (pp. 56–86). Oxford, U.K.: Blackwell.

Chisholm, L., & Kovacheva, S. (2002). *Exploring the European youth mosaic: The social situation of young people in Europe.* Strasbourg: Council of Europe Publishing.

Couch, C. (1999). *Social change in western Europe.* Oxford, U.K.: Oxford University Press.

Dey, I., & Morris, S. (1999). Parental support for young adults in Europe. *Children and Youth Services Review, 21*(11/12), 915–935.

Drew, E., Emerek, R., & Mahon, E. (1998). *Women, work and the family in Europe.* London: Routledge.

Edwards, R. (2004). Present and absent in troubling ways: Families and social capital debates. *Sociological Review, 52*(1), 1-21.

Edwards R., Franklin, J., & Holland, J. (2003). *Families and social capital: Exploring the issues.* London: South Bank University.

European Commission (2003). *Building the knowledge society: Social and human capital interactions.* Commission staff working paper SEC 2003, 652. Brussels: European Commission.

Gallie, D., & Paugam, S. (Eds.) (2000). *Welfare regimes and the experience of unemployment in Europe.* Oxford, U.K.: Oxford University Press.

Gangl, M. (2001). European patterns of labour market entry: A dichotomy of occupationalized versus non-occupationalized systems? *European Societies, 3,* 471–494.

Hantrais, L. (2004). *Family policy matters: Responding to family change in Europe.* Bristol: Policy Press.

Holdsworth, C., & Morgan, M. (2005). *Transitions in context: Leaving home, independence and adulthood.* Maidenhead, U.K.: Open University Press.

Iacovou, M. (2001). *Leaving home in the European Union* (ISER working paper 2001-18). Colchester, U.K.: University of Essex, Institute for Social and Economic Research.

Iacovou, M., & Berthoud, R. (2001). *Young people's lives: A map of Europe.* Colchester, U.K.: University of Essex, Institute for Social and Economic Research.

Jones, G. (2005). *The thinking and behaviour of young adults (aged 16–25): Literature review for the Social Exclusion Unit.* London: Social Exclusion Unit.

Kaufmann, F.-X., Knijsten, A., Schulze, H-J., & Strohmeier, K. P. (2002). *Family life and family policies in Europe: Problems and issues in comparative perspective* (Vol. 2). Oxford, U.K.: Oxford University Press.

Mihailova, D. (2004). *Social capital in central and eastern Europe: A critical assessment and literature review.* Budapest: Center for Policy Studies.

Mitev, P.-E. (2005). *The new young: Bulgarian youth and the European perspective.* Sofia: East-West.

Morrow, V. (1999). Conceptualising social capital in relation to the well-being of children and young people: A critical review. *Sociological Review, 47*(4), 744–765.

Müller, W., & Gangl, M. (2003). *Transitions from education to work in Europe: The integration of youth into EU labour markets.* Oxford, U.K.: Oxford University Press.

Müller, W., & Shavit, Y. (1997). *From school to work: A comparative study of educational qualifications and occupational destinations.* Oxford, U.K.: Oxford University Press.

Sgritta, G. (1999, Oct.). *Too late, too slow: The difficult process of becoming an adult in Italy.* Paper presented at the International Jacobs Foundation Conference "The Transition to Adulthood: Explaining National Differences," Communication Centre Marbach Castle, Marbach, Switzerland.

Sgritta, G. (2001). Family and welfare systems in the transition to adulthood: An emblematic case study. In *Family Forms and the Young Generation in Europe.* Report on the Annual Seminar of the European Observatory for the Social Situation, Demography and Family (pp. 59–87). Vienna: Austrian Institute for Family Studies.

Shavit, Y., & Blossfeld, H.-P. (Eds.) (1993). *Persistent inequality: Changing educational attainment in thirteen countries.* Boulder, CO: Westview.

Ule, M., & Rener, T. (Eds.) (1998). *Youth in Slovenia: New perspectives from the nineties.* Ljubljana, Slovenia: Youth Department.
van de Velde, C. (2001). *Autonomy construction in a dependence situation: Young unemployed people and family relationships in France and Spain.* Paper presented at the International Conference on "Family Forms and the Young Generation in Europe," University of Milano-Bicocca, Milan.
Wallace, C., & Kovatcheva, S. (1998). *Youth in society: The construction and deconstruction of youth in east and west Europe.* London: Macmillan.

ANDREW BIGGART is a lecturer in education at Queen's University Belfast. His main research interests center on low-attainment, postcompulsory education and training and young people's transitions from education to work.

SIYKA KOVACHEVA is a lecturer in sociology at the University of Plovdiv, Bulgaria. Her current research focuses on youth citizenship, labor market integration, and family formation.

6

In this chapter, the author argues for the essential role of "doing gender" in the transition of young people from education to the labor market. Two relevant concepts are introduced: biographicity and gender competence. They are illustrated with a female and a male case.

Biography and Gender in Youth Transitions

Barbara Stauber

The gender issue is not as self-evident as it has been in past decades when youth sociologists and educationalists were concerned about female disadvantage in education, vocational training, and the labor market. The long-term effect of educational reforms in Europe in the late 1960s and early 1970s, which showed girls dominating educational achievement, brought up doubts whether gender should still be considered a category of social structuration. Gender seemed to share the same fate as the categories of social class and race. The former master status of these categories became a highly contended issue, especially in youth transitions (Furlong & Cartmel, 1997). However, questions have been raised if late-modern conditions could blur still-existing social inequalities (see the proceedings of the European Sociological Association, 2005) and may possibly modernize gender hierarchies but not abolish them.

It is obvious that both genders represent heterogeneous groups and that differences are partly bigger within the gender groups than between them. Therefore, the question of how much gender matters can be clarified empirically only by looking at specific groups of young women and men and how they are affected by gender-related structures, ascriptions, and experiences. Structure-related considerations must evolve to include new gender discourses that claim that gender, instead of being a given, is to be understood as a bipolar and hierarchical social construction. This constructivist turn is especially relevant in considering youth transitions as seismographs for social change (Bjerrum Nielsen, 1996; Griffin, 1993; Wyn & White, 1997).

NEW DIRECTIONS FOR CHILD AND ADOLESCENT DEVELOPMENT, no. 113, Fall 2006   © Wiley Periodicals, Inc.
Published online in Wiley InterScience (www.interscience.wiley.com) • DOI: 10.1002/cad.169

However, constructivist approaches, which were developed in the United States in the late 1960s and during the 1970s, were first recognized in Europe only in the beginning of the 1990s. Concepts for a new perspective on the (re)production of gender and gender relationships in everyday life had long been developed by ethno-methodologists such as Garfinkel (1967), Goffman (1977), and Kessler and McKenna (1978), but it needed the influence of U.S.-American philosopher and gender theorist Butler (1990) to set a change in paradigms in motion. With a time lag of about 20 years, the social construction of gender became the dominant formula of European gender studies. This introduced a gendered division of labor in capitalist societies that *produced* a bipolar and hierarchical gender order that, in daily agency, is (re)*produced* again and again.

Thinking in gender differences came under the suspicion of *reification*: taking the outcomes of social processes as something quasi-natural. Meanwhile, it belongs to the standard statements in European books on (female) gender studies, distancing it from reifying difference and concentrating instead on processes of *differentiation* (Fenstermaker, West, & Zimmerman, 1991). The new subdiscipline of men's studies entered the discourse only a few years ago and could benefit from these constructivist considerations right from the start (Connell, 1995).

My contribution will shed light on the late-modern complexity of gendered biographical transitions. It is driven by the search for methodological solutions to deal with the topic of gendered transitions. I begin with findings concerning mechanisms of "doing gender" in transitions, discuss methodological consequences, and briefly consider the biographical approach. I continue with two concepts that are becoming more essential to research on youth transitions: *biographicity* and *gender competences.* I will give two examples of gender-sensitive research on youth transitions from the recently accomplished YOYO research project (see Chapter One in this volume for further details) to show the analytical potential of these concepts. The young people's statements included in this contribution all derive from the YOYO project. The chapter closes with an outlook into future research on gendered (youth) transitions and transition biographies of young women and men.

Doing Gender in Youth Transitions

Transitions from school to work mark a decisive status passage in female and male life courses in which young women and men shape their present and future biographies. The fact that these transitions still have a gendered character can be explained only by approaches that take different coproducers and mechanisms of doing gender into account. Regarding education, gender no longer accounts for female disadvantage. In all Organisation for Economic Co-operation and Development (OECD) countries, the participation of girls in education is better than that of their male counter-

NEW DIRECTIONS FOR CHILD AND ADOLESCENT DEVELOPMENT • DOI: 10.1002/cad

parts on all educational levels. Girls' dropout rates are lower than those of boys. Girls receive better marks, write better exams, and on average achieve a higher educational status. Yet, when they pass into the labor market, their educational advantages turn into disadvantages: their educational achievements do not pay off to the same extent as do those of their male competitors but, on the contrary, produce a worse position. This phenomenon can be explained by two interwoven mechanisms: *presorting* and *postsorting*.

By comparing different European gender regimes, Smyth (2002) identified significant presorting by the educational system through female vocational tracking. An evaluation of transnational studies that included European Union (EU)–member states, Canada, the United States, and Japan showed that participation levels in postcompulsory education are higher among young women than among young men. "However, gender differences persist when type of education/training is considered, with females more likely to enter 'general' rather than 'vocational' tracks and to take gender-typed vocational courses" (Hannan, Raffe, & Smyth, 1996, p. 11). These gendered tracks lead to educational achievements with a different labor market value: educational capital achieved in "typical female" tracks cannot be converted into profitable careers to the same extent as that from "typical male" tracks.

Regarding postsorting through the occupational system, Smyth (2002) in her evaluation of European countries with different gender regimes (Austria, the Netherlands, Sweden, Finland, France, Belgium, Greece, Hungary, Slovenia, Romania, and Slovakia) could show that "there is very little gender differentiation in labour market integration in the Scandinavian countries, the Netherlands and the Eastern European countries (with the exception of Slovakia). In contrast, there are very marked gender differences evident in Belgium and the Mediterranean countries. These differences are not explained by gender differences in educational level, field of education or family status. In fact, the gender gap increases when these factors are taken into account" (p. 10).

These studies show that gender is still codetermined by *structures*, such as gendered educational tracks and gendered options to amortize educational capital on the labor markets. On the other hand, these structures work only by institutional and personal *agency*, which validates gendered ascriptions and regulations and thus reproduces gender. Especially today's young women live in a world of contradictory messages: Despite official requests for females to opt for nontypical vocational routes, many of them still make the experience of being channeled by representatives of institutions such as the employment services into gendered routes. As 17-year-old Mona from Germany put it when we interviewed her about her choices for a vocational career, "In secondary school, they only offer for the girls hairdressing, retail, and child-care, or even less, only retail and hairdressing."

Personal experience refers here to *institutionally situated processes of doing gender*, conflicting with the life plans this young woman had at the beginning of her transition trajectory.

New Directions for Child and Adolescent Development • DOI: 10.1002/cad

Doing gender can hardly be explained by young women's and men's self-concepts: as is shown in their professional orientation, most young women and men are interested in a professional career. Former gender differences have blended in. Thinking about their future, both young women and men on almost all educational levels want to have a good job and a family of their own. As demonstrated by European research, differences *within* the genders in professional orientation are bigger than *between* them (Scherer, 2003). However, by dealing with the occupational options they effectively have, by recognizing the (gendered) possibilities to amortize their educational investments, young women and men—willingly or not—succumb to the gendered features of their own transitions.

Insight into the dynamics of doing gender is provided by biographical research. The dealing with contradictions, ambivalences, structural barriers, and opportunities is a powerful vector in generating gender differences, starting from institutional acknowledgment, given or withheld support, to the level of reliable or misleading opportunity structures for realizing different life plans. On all these levels, young women and men still have different experiences: Glass ceilings are still more a female experience, whereas young men are more likely to step into glass escalators, even more so when young couples build families (European Commission, 2005). Late-modern ideology of individualization in tandem with the myth of modern gender equality turns gendered experiences into personal deficiencies or success, thereby reinforcing gender-"specific" explanations.

The interplay of these mechanisms and individual consequences young women and men draw from them—that is, the social construction of doing gender—can become visible by such biographical approaches. They bring into consideration that gender can also be seen as a resource for creating a sense of coherence in young people's lives (Antonovsky, 1987) and for individual *identity work* dealing with self-explanation and meaning attribution (Bjerrum Nielsen, 1996; Frosh, Phoenix, & Pattman, 2002). Such identity work becomes increasingly important against the backdrop of contingency, insecurity, and uncertainty in the transition biographies of young people in late modernity (Giddens, 1991; Zinn, 2005).

The Biographical Approach

Most data collections, certainly on youth transitions, give information about the outcomes of decisions, not so much about the decision *making*. The outcomes of school-to-work transitions are often taken as the expression of young women's and men's intentions, which is a wrong supposition. If not explicitly ascertained, we know nothing about initial intentions or about influencing factors and experiences during transition processes. Assuming that such processes consist of different layers of experiences and that only by reconstructing these processes do we get information about doing gender, gender-sensitive research must apply methods that are appropriate to reconstruct such processes. This means that to do research on educational and work transitions, methodological designs need to be developed by which in-depth knowledge is gained about how subjective experiences and processes of reinforcement or discouragement influence individual strategies and the decision making of young women and men.

Being open to subjective relevance and meaning attribution of the young people themselves means being susceptible to their "first-order constructions." Such constructions are the basis for making scientific interpretations as "second-order constructions," as stressed by the *biographical approach.* This perspective has become widely recognized in Europe since the seventies in social research in general but especially in gender studies (Apitzsch & Kontos, 2003; Curti, 1998; Leccardi, 1996) and youth sociology (Alheit, 1994; Bloomer & Hodkinson, 2000; Heinz, 1999; Reiter, 2003; Thomson, Bell, Henderson, Holland, McGrellis, & Sharpe, 2002). Chamberlayne, Bornat, and Wengraf (2000) even speak of a "turn to biographical methods in social science." This approach criticizes a positivistic understanding of social phenomena and takes into serious account what feminists have demanded for social research and practice: the dimension of subjective experience. Epistemologically, the roots of the biographical approach lay in symbolic interactionism, pragmatism, and the Chicago school that, as a common feature, have a dialectic, and not a dualistic, understanding of the relationship between individual and society. This allows for a critical reconstruction of processes in which all dimensions of "doing difference" can be deconstructed and respectively reconstructed. The biographical approach with open interview methods gives women and men space to do this reconstruction themselves through reflection on their lives; however, its analytical interest is not restricted to individual agency but concerns the interplay of structure and agency: It takes biographies as "radical documents of 'sociality'" (Apitzsch, 1990, p. 13).

Although there are legitimate critiques pointing to the fact that biographical research methods have been applied above all in Europe (and in Germany, see Hitzler, 2005), social research that makes use of personal accounts and narratives is becoming an increasingly international phenomenon (Miller, 2005; see also International Sociological Association Research Committee 38: Biography and Society), albeit with different emphasis (Flick, 2005). However, it would be misleading to equate the turn toward biographies with a turn away from structural analysis. Rather, the well-known dualisms between subject-object, structure-agency, demand-coping, and so on are left behind. This points again to the link between the biographical perspective, which gives room for (young) people themselves to reconstruct their social reality and biography, and social constructivism, which is interested in the social modes and processes of how gender, ethnicity, and difference in general are done. This link makes the biographical approach and respective methods (Chamberlayne, Bornat, & Apitzsch, 2004) all the more compatible for reconstructive social (gender) research and reconnects it with its roots (Dausien, 2000).

Biographicity and Gender Competences: Two Key Competencies in Late-Modern Transitions

For today's research in youth transitions, two concepts become increasingly essential. Both of them result from a biographical perspective on fragmented and insecure youth transitions and the increasing demand of "biographical work" to cope with these uncertainties.

The first concept, biographicity, points to the self-referential ability of modern individuals to integrate new and sometimes puzzling experiences in their biography (Alheit & Dausien, 2000) and to associate with this new knowledge. It is a way to produce coherence in the context of increasingly fragmented transitions. Biographicity identifies the social principles of how individual experiences are organized and can be enlarged. It points to a generative structure for biographical and social reality that itself results from selection processes the individual has made in the course of time—for example, in education and other social contexts. This kind of biographical reflexivity is not simply a resource; rather, the questions are how it is produced, how it functions, and how it can be facilitated by appropriate (educational) settings. Consequently, biographicity became an important concept in the European discourses on lifelong learning. In the broad debate about key competencies in the context of the OECD, which roughly distinguishes three categories: social competencies, self-competencies, and methodological competencies (Rychen & Salganik, 2003), biographicity can be regarded as a basic self-competence to deal with late-modern transition demands.

Biographicity refers to the individual's capacity of reworking and transforming intersubjective knowledge, to which all kinds of gendered information belong. This is the link to the second key concept: gender competence, pointing to subjective awareness about gendered role models, gendering ascriptions, gendered delegation of tasks, and so on. It refers to a certain level of reflexivity, which would imply some sensitivity for daily interactions in which all these subtle "genderisms" take place. Considering doing gender as a result of the interplay of structure and agency, or better, as situated agency, it becomes clear how competent handling with all kinds of gendered information and ascriptions relates to biographicity. Without overemphasizing the gender issue and being aware that gender is only one of several dimensions of social positioning, besides social class, ethnicity, and so on (Smith, 1998), gender competence could be defined as learning to handle contradictory demands in male and female life courses, to decode gendered ascriptions, and to deal with them, not only by using them but also by refusing them in order to construct one's own gender identity. It represents another key dimension in social and self-competencies.

The common feature of biographicity and gender competence is *reflexivity*—that is, about the way one's own (gendered) biography is constructed. The concepts basically imply a reconstructive perspective. Interviews—all the more if they include narrative parts—are instruments to set such reflexive reconstruction in motion. Biographicity and gender competence not only are useful guiding perspectives in transition research, they also are *promoted* by (biographical) research methods appropriate to initiate biographical reflections (Frosh et al., 2002; Schittenhelm, 2005). In our own research, we, too, made use of such methods, as I will illustrate with two examples in the following section.

Two Cases from the YOYO Project

The YOYO project analyzed the impact of (biographical) participation on young people's (de)motivation to engage in their school-to-work transitions (see also Chapter 7). The project concentrated on young people who, as a consequence of frustrating experiences with institutional settings and the labor market, had resigned from active engagement in their transitions to work. These young people have been accessed in projects selected as "best practice" regarding participatory approaches in support for school-to-work transitions. We interviewed them at their entrance in the project and a second time one-and-a-half years later when they were about to leave the project and transit to further education or work, or failed to do so. Our design allowed for a biographical perspective on the life course of these young people (for a full account, see Walther, du Bois-Reymond, & Biggart, 2006).

The first case is part of the West German study. It concerns a training scheme for young women with a migration background. Germany is famous for its dual training system that combines a school-based curriculum with practical training in enterprises and companies. Yet, many young people do not find training places because of structural changes in the production sector that lead to severe shortages of training places. It is exactly in the respective segments of the labor market where gender is done with high evidence: whereas male applicants with bad marks still get training places in "male" sectors such as construction, female applicants are deferred to "waiting loops" in schools or training measures they did not have a chance to choose themselves. La Silhouette is a training project that gives young female migrants from lower educational levels the opportunity to qualify in tailoring. Besides offering training places, the project establishes a female space that is meant to stimulate the creativity of young women and empower them to think about their life chances in new ways. The project acknowledges their different cultural roots: for example, when using the different cultural origins of its participants as a pool for new fashion ideas. It encourages young women to create bridges between their culture of origin and the social context they are living in; they learn to negotiate culture. After the training, La Silhouette accompanies the young women to the labor markets, operating a well-established network that includes the chamber of crafts and local companies.

One of the former participants we interviewed, Sevdiye, is 22 years old and the daughter of Turkish immigrants. She has lived with her family in

Munich, Germany, since her early childhood. As one of the oldest of six children, she has been responsible for her younger siblings from early childhood on. Gendered household tasks are normal in Turkish families. Sevdiye describes her father as being rather strict, and when it came to her vocational training decision, it was he who decided that she would take over his profession as a dressmaker and one day accompany him to Turkey as his assistant. La Silhouette's focus on tailoring, along with its single-sex structure, was ultimately the reason her father entered her into the project. Sevdiye finished her training at La Silhouette two years ago. She frequently returns for visits and to use the equipment. She also volunteers at her former training site. When we talked to her, she was preparing the choreography for the next fashion show along with the current trainee class. Looking back at her transitional biography, she talks about her time in the project as a phase that helped her to come out of her "shell"—a period of personal empowerment. Asked what the training has given her, she responds without hesitating for a moment: "Self-esteem . . . first of all: self-esteem. And autonomy. Also creativity. To develop myself. You simply have learned how to proceed in life, after all. Optimism!"

With this statement, Sevdiye relates her empowering experiences to the period she had endured before, which she reconstructs as being full of external and internal difficulties: "Before starting training at La Silhouette, I was supershy and without any self-esteem. Locked within myself. . . . And this is the worst thing which could happen to a woman, I think: being without self-esteem."

The following quote shows her awareness about her new self-consciousness and the new options of another female life, as has been foreseen for her by her cultural and family background: "If I had not developed this self-confidence, I would be married long ago, would have children long ago, but all this I have been given: this ability to assert myself, to say: no, I simply will not do that! What they [the social worker from La Silhouette] have given me, I only noticed afterwards. And I developed it further, and then I got this idea of power-woman, and I said to myself: I move out, now it's time!"

To her, the turn to another female concept is not an individual project but a common endeavor of the group of young trainees and the female project leaders: "This only came with time (and) by support of La Silhouette. This has been for us a real home. After a while, I could talk about things which I even could not discuss with my siblings, it was simply gigantic, this cohesion [in the project]." Sevdiye has been living on her own and with her boyfriend for four years. She has several side jobs and works toward her master course as a fashion designer.

The second example is from the Italian study. ArciRagazzi, a youth association organizing leisure and cultural activities, provides young people, especially those who are living in deprived neighborhoods or are coming from detention centers, with life perspectives beyond unemployment. It prevents involvement with the mafia, an option for many unemployed

NEW DIRECTIONS FOR CHILD AND ADOLESCENT DEVELOPMENT • DOI: 10.1002/cad

young men. In southern Italy, youth unemployment reaches 60 percent, and young people have to endure long waiting periods before they get a chance to enter a regular job. ArciRagazzi has a strong community approach. It initiates career orientation, helps with transition to work, and stimulates young entrepreneurship, which in Italy is a viable route for youth transitions.

Paolo, 19 years old, from Palermo (Sicily) has been at severe risk of getting involved in criminal activities because of his brother's history of drug addiction and detention in a juvenile reformatory. After starting a rehabilitation program, his brother convinced Paolo to join ArciRagazzi. The project operators described Paolo as lazy and apathetic at the beginning, but he slowly became involved in community activities and even brought some of his friends with him. His first encounter with the project challenged his macho attitude, a normal part of the socialization in his milieu: "My first activity day in the project was on Carnival Day at the recreation center in Borgonuovo with little children. I really felt ridiculous because we were all made up. It seemed to me a strange thing, and I asked myself: What happens if a friend of mine comes along and sees me with this makeup? What will he think of me?"

Paolo started to organize activities in the children's recreational center and became the main editor of the association's newsletter. Through project workers, he got in touch with young people who operated a music band. He started studying guitar and eventually was in charge of the music sector of the association. He began to write the lyrics and music for socially committed songs in Sicilian dialect. At the same time, he is a member in a band that performs both in the association shows and city festivals. His involvement has allowed him to recognize his musical interest. He hopes to continue working with music and songs. He says, "I think it's important to rediscover the Sicilian musical tradition. Look at the TV: they pass off our Sicilian language as a dialect. I want to recover the Sicilian language and show that it's possible to write songs in this language. And then I also want to work with children as an animator."

Music has helped Paolo to find meaning in life; he managed to extend the options offered by the project to develop his interest further: he performs, and he gets enthusiastic feedback. At present, he is earning his living by working irregularly in the transport sector. This job takes up a lot of his time and energy, but he still sticks to his new life goals: "I learned so much, especially working with children, and that's what I want to do in the future."

Interpretations and Methodological Consequences

Sevdiye reconstructs her personal development, from the shy little Turkish girl she has been to the tough young woman she is now. Besides enjoying some staginess of her story, she makes an important link: she presents her personal growth as gendered identity work, including her own interpretation of what being a woman means to her.

With dressmaking and designing, she has found relevance in her present and for her future life, something that meets her longing for creative work, challenges her endurance, and gives her a clear goal of what she wants to do in life. Considering the cultural norms and practices of her family background, she has definitely left the route that was foreseen for her.

Once having overcome the first threshold of (gendered) embarrassment, Paulo became engaged in doing volunteer work with children. He learned to value other sources of acknowledgment. Rather than being respected by his peers for macho behavior, he received acknowledgment for social engagement and above all for being a musician. When reconstructing the biographical relevance of his new experiences as a social activist, educator for young children, singer, and guitar player in the interview, the gender subtext of his biographical work appears; with these new activities, he created new options for construing masculinity that are expressed above all in his future plans to work with children. This prospect is a sharp contrast to the gendered route toward which he was previously heading.

The examples of these two young people show how biographicity and gender competence work in personal progress: Both Sevdiye and Paolo show a high level of competence to integrate new and puzzling experiences into their biographical contexts. They learned to understand that contradictions and ambivalences belong to (transition) biographies, and they rose to the challenge of integrating new experiences.

For Sevdiye and Paolo, these new experiences had a strong gender dimension: Both young adults "gained" biographicity through leaving the gendered routes suggested to them by their families and dominant cultural norms and values of the milieus they live in. Both had the opportunity to experiment with different gender roles and actively made use of these opportunities.

There are differences with regard to the level of reflexivity on which gender competence is achieved. Where Sevdiye explicitly reflects on how her gender role would have normally been defined and how she diverges from that, Paolo seems to leave the normal pathways of a young Sicilian man in his social context simply by doing: by working with children, exploring new fields of experience, and finding meaningfulness and acknowledgment of new persons, adults, and peers. Besides the fact that Sevdiye is some years older than Paolo, gender is obviously differently dealt with by their different learning contexts: Whereas in La Silhouette the gender issue is one explicit topic of the project discourse, the supposed gender-neutral working principle of ArciRagazzi is learning by experimenting.

This refers to the relevance of opportunity structures for reflection, in both pedagogical and research settings. In this regard, biographical research methods have a double advantage: by inspiring young people to look back to a certain period of their life, these methods generate subjective narrations that on the one hand make visible their processes of meaning making. On the other hand, competencies such as biographicity and gender competence are promoted by such opportunities. It has been the experience of our research, as of other studies using such methods, that spaces for reflection beyond everyday life are aggressively used by young people to reframe experiences and to reconstruct their transitional biography together with their gender biography.

The two examples also show the relevance of social contexts that allow for creating new (gender) behaviors as fields for such transition research. It is of methodological interest to explore not only "normal gender settings" but also contexts that allow for doing gender in a different way. This could be cultural youth work, media pedagogy, and other nonformal learning settings. It could be projects that explicitly focus on "different gender policies" (such as La Silhouette) but also projects (such as ArciRagazzi), which have only an implicit gender dimension, simply offering new fields of experiences to young women and men. This means: taking into account that what young women and men could learn depends on facilitating structures for learning and on making space for different experiences.

References

Alheit, P. (1994). *Taking the knocks: Youth unemployment and biography—A qualitative analysis.* London: Cassel.

Alheit, P., & Dausien, B. (2000). "Biographicity" as a basic resource of lifelong learning. In P. Alheit (Ed.), *Lifelong learning inside and outside of schools* (pp. 400–422). Roskilde, Denmark: Roskilde University, Universität Bremen, and University of Leeds. Retrieved December 14, 2005, from http://www.erill.uni-bremen.de/lios/sections/s4 alheit.html.

Antonovsky, A. (1987). *Unraveling the mystery of health: How people manage stress and stay well.* San Francisco: Jossey-Bass.

Apitzsch, U. (1990). *Lernbiographien zwischen den Kulturen* [Learning biographies between the cultures]. Paper given at the 12th Conference of the German Educational Research Association, Frankfurt.

Apitzsch, U., & Kontos, M. (Eds.) (2003). Self-employment: Gender—Migration. *International Review of Sociology, 13*(1), 183–204.

Bjerrum Nielsen, H. (1996). The magic writing pad: On gender and identity work. *Young: Nordic Journal of Youth Research, 4*(3), 2–18.

Bloomer, M., & Hodkinson, P. (2000). Learning careers: Continuity and change in young people's dispositions to learning. *British Educational Research Journal, 26*(5), 583–597.

Butler, J. (1990). *Gender trouble: Feminism and the subversion of identity.* London: Routledge.

Chamberlayne, P., Bornat, J., & Apitzsch, U. (2004). *Biographical methods and professional practice: An international perspective.* Bristol: Policy Press.

Chamberlayne, P., Bornat, J., & Wengraf, T. (Eds.) (2000). *The turn to biographical methods in social science: Comparative issues and examples.* London: Routledge.

Connell, B. (1995). *Masculinities.* Cambridge, U.K.: Polity Press.

Curti, L. (1998). *Female stories, female bodies: Narrative, identity and representation.* London: Macmillan.

Dausien, B. (2000, March). *Biography, learning and the construction of gender.* Paper presented at the European Society for Research on Education of Adults, Biography Network Gender, Learning and Biography Conference, Roskilde, Denmark. Abstract retrieved January 12, 2006, from http://www.evu.ruc.dk/eng/events/papers/bettina. html.

European Commission (2005). *Report on equality between women and men.* Brussels: European Commission.

European Sociological Association (2005). Rethinking inequalities. Presented at the 7th biannual conference, Torun, Poland. Retrieved January 15, 2006, from http://www.7thesaconference.umk.pl/index1.php.

Fenstermaker, S., West, C., & Zimmerman, D. (1991). Gender inequality: New conceptual terrain. In R. Lesser-Blumberg (Ed.), *Gender, family and economy: The triple overlap* (pp. 236–249). Newbury Park, CA: Sage.

Flick, U. (2005). *Qualitative research in sociology in Germany and the US: State of the art, differences and developments.* Forum: Qualitative Social Research, 6, 3, Art. 23. Retrieved October 11, 2005, from http://www.qualitative-research.net/fqs-texte/3–05/05–3–23-e_p.html.

Frosh, S., Phoenix, A., & Pattman, R. (2002). *Young masculinities.* London: Palgrave.

Furlong, A., & Cartmel, F. (1997). *Young people and social change: Individualization and risk in late modernity.* Buckingham, U.K.: Open University Press.

Garfinkel, H. (1967). *Studies in ethnomethodology.* Englewood Cliffs, NJ: Prentice-Hall.

Giddens, A. (1991). *Modernity and self-identity: Self and society in the late modern age.* Cambridge, U.K.: Polity Press.

Goffman, E. (1977). The arrangement between the sexes. *Theory and Society, 4,* 301–331.

Griffin, C. (1993). *Representations of youth.* Cambridge, U.K.: Blackwell.

Hannan, D. F., Raffe, D., & Smyth, E. (1996). *Cross-national research on school to work transitions: An analytical framework.* Organisation for Economic Co-operation and Development paper. Abstract retrieved October 11, 2005, from http://www.oecd.org/dataoecd/39/59/1925587.pdf.

Heinz, W. R. (Ed.) (1999). *From education to work: Cross-national perspectives.* New York: Cambridge University Press.

Hitzler, R. (2005). *The reconstruction of meaning: Notes on German interpretive sociology.* Forum: Qualitative Social Research, 6, 3, Art. 45. Retrieved October 11, 2005, from http://www.qualitative-research.net/fqs-texte/3–05/05–3–45-e_p.html.

Kessler, S. J., & McKenna, W. (1978). *Gender: An ethnomethodological approach.* New York: Wiley.

Leccardi, C. (1996). *Futuro breve: Le giovani donne e il futuro* [Short future: Young women and the future]. Turin, Italy: Rosenberg & Sellier.

Miller, R. L. (Ed.) (2005). *Biographical research methods: A four volume set.* London: Sage.

Reiter, H. (2003). Past, present, future: Biographical time structuring of disadvantaged young people. *Young, 11*(3), 253–279.

Rychen, D. S., & Salganik, L. H. (Eds.) (2003). *Key competencies for a successful life and a well functioning society.* Göttingen, Germany: Hogrefe & Huber.

Scherer, S. (2003). *Work and family: Literature review for the ChangEqual network.* Retrieved October 11, 2005, from http://www.nuff.ox.ac.uk/projects/ChangeQual/papers/public/themes/1/theme_1_378_WorkandFamilyJuly.pdf.

Schittenhelm, K. (2005). *Soziale lagen im übergang* [Social positions in transition]. Wiesbaden, Germany: VS-Verlag.

Smith, V. (1998). *Not just race, not just gender: Black feminist readings.* London: Routledge.

Smyth, E. (2002). Gender differentiation and early labor market integration across Europe. In I. Kogan & W. Müller (Eds.), *School-to-work transitions in Europe: Analyses of the EU labor force survey 2000.* Mannheim, Germany: Mannheim Centre for European Social Research.

Thomson, R., Bell, R., Henderson, S., Holland, J., McGrellis, S., & Sharpe, S. (2002). Critical moments: Choice, chance and opportunity in young people's narratives of transition to adulthood. *Sociology, 36*(2), 335–354.

Walther, A., du Bois-Reymond, M., & Biggart, A. (Eds.) (2006). *Participation in transition? The motivation of young people for working and learning in Europe.* Frankfurt am Main: Lang.

Wyn, J., & White, R. (1997). *Rethinking youth.* London: Sage.

Zinn, J. (2005). Biographical certainty in reflexive modernity. In N. Kelly, C. Horrocks, K. Milnes, B. Roberts, & D. Robinson (Eds.), *Narrative, memory and everyday life.* Huddersfield, U.K.: Huddersfield University.

BARBARA STAUBER is senior researcher at the Institute for Regional Innovation and Social Research (IRIS), Tübingen, Germany, and at the Tübingen Institute for Gender Studies. Her current research focuses on youth cultures, young parenthood, and biographical transitions in a gender perspective.

NEW DIRECTIONS FOR CHILD AND ADOLESCENT DEVELOPMENT • DOI: 10.1002/cad

7

This chapter deals with a fundamental change in young people's transitions to work. Flexible labor markets have led to a diversification of transition patterns, but policy measures are unresponsive to the needs and aspirations of young people. New risks and challenges emerge that are addressed differently in the different European societies.

Transitions from School to Work in Europe: Destandardization and Policy Trends

Andreas Walther, Wim Plug

During the past decades, the transformation from industrial to postindustrial economies has changed the context of young people's transition to the labor market. In most western countries, these transitions have become not only prolonged but also more fragmented, diversified, and less linear. They can be compared with yo-yos as they go back and forth between education, employment, and unemployment. The destandardization of youth transitions has replaced security and predictability by personal choices and risks. Based on a concept that perceives social integration as the dialectic of structure and agency, we analyze youth transitions from a dual perspective by relating education and labor market conditions to the subjective perspective and agency of individuals. Some of our ideas are based on findings obtained in the YOYO project,[1] which studied the motivational careers of young people in their transitions from school to work and the potentials of participation and informal learning in young people's transitions. The project involved ten European countries (Bulgaria, Denmark, Germany, Ireland, Italy, Netherlands, Portugal, Romania, Spain, and the United Kingdom). The two milestones were biographical interviews with young people on their transition experiences and case studies into projects addressing school-to-work-transitions in a participatory way (Walther, du Bois-Reymond, & Biggart, 2006). In the first part of this chapter, we outline some of the implications from a biographical perspective of the destandardization of youth

NEW DIRECTIONS FOR CHILD AND ADOLESCENT DEVELOPMENT, no. 113, Fall 2006   © Wiley Periodicals, Inc.
Published online in Wiley InterScience (www.interscience.wiley.com) • DOI: 10.1002/cad.170

transitions. In the subsequent section, we provide empirical evidence for the diversification of young Europeans' transition patterns and show that a smooth transition to the labor market and economic independence is only one of many possible paths. Then we analyze European policy discourses and trends relating to these diversified transition patterns, paying special attention to the group of disadvantaged youth and variations across different *transition regimes* in Europe. A plea for more theoretical and practical work concludes the chapter.

Destandardization: From Linear Toward Yo-Yo Transitions

Historically, the "invention of youth" is located at the wake of modernity and associated with the institutionalization of the life course. The more paid work became the central mode of social integration and the backbone of individual life courses, the more necessary became a preparatory phase of education (Musgrove, 1964). The development of national education systems and welfare states resulted in a normal life-course regime (Kohli, 1985) that comprised three life stages, namely education, employment, and retirement. However, as a result of women's double socialization with regard to work and family, female life courses have always been more differentiated than suggested by assumptions of normality. Especially in the Fordist period, normal life courses promised happiness—though on different socioeconomic levels—and guaranteed social integration for those who followed institutionally established patterns (Myles, 1991).

The post-Fordist flexibilization of production and socioeconomic and sociocultural individualization have rendered stable life phases and predictable status passages less reliable. The prolongation of educational trajectories has gone hand in hand with an increasing number of alternations between education, training, and work. As a consequence, transitions between youth and adulthood involve higher risks of social exclusion. In the European Union,

- *Youth unemployment figures* are twice as high as those for adults, with one of ten persons aged 15 to 24 years being unemployed (and one of five among the economically active ones but with regional variations ranging from 4 percent in Austria to 70 percent in southern Italy) while more and more young people work under precarious conditions with fixed-term contracts (European Commission, 2005).
- *Early school leaving* (one of six leaves school without a postcompulsory certificate) reflects both unequal social backgrounds and the uncertainty of whether educational investments will pay off (European Commission, 2005).
- There is a noticeable *mismatch* between outdated qualifications and the rapidly changing demands of the labor market (Müller & Gangl, 2003).

NEW DIRECTIONS FOR CHILD AND ADOLESCENT DEVELOPMENT • DOI: 10.1002/cad

- A constantly high share of young people (estimated around 5 percent to 10 percent)—the "status zero" group (Williamson, 1997)—are neither in employment, education, or training nor registered unemployed.

Destandardization also implies that the assumed coincidence between structure and agency, the institutionalized life-course trajectories and their subjective appropriation by individuals in constructing their biographies, are no longer self-evident (Giddens, 1984). More and more young people have to make individual decisions about their lives without having reliable collective markers of orientation. This "biographization" trend (Alheit & Dausien, 2000) is also due to the fragmentation of transitions inasmuch as adult-status features—work, family, and citizenship—are no longer achieved as a package but follow different rationales and rhythms that have to be reconciled individually, with gendered implications of becoming a man or woman. Whereas addressing youth transitions is constitutive for labor societies, it is reductive in terms of transitions to work. Hence, the metaphor of yo-yo transitions refers not only to the growing reversibility of transitions between youth and adulthood but also to the fact that young people increasingly experience periods in which they are confronted with contradicting social expectations in different spheres of life—be it as youngsters or adults—while they subjectively feel they are somewhere in between these two stages (Pais, 2000; European Group for Integrated Social Research, 2001; Plug, Zeijl, & du Bois-Reymond, 2003). The destandardization of transitions goes hand in hand with individualization. More and more young people have to make individual decisions and are individually held responsible for them although resources and opportunities remain unequally distributed. In fact, yo-yo transitions are not necessarily young people's choice; they are frequently imposed on them by such traditional structures of social inequality as class and education, gender, ethnicity, or region. However, inequality takes new forms of disadvantage. For those with restricted economic, cultural, and social capital, a normal biography still stands for a "decent life." However, a growing number of young people have to reorient themselves once they discover that the likelihood of realizing a normal life course has decreased and that they do not have sufficient resources to stand competition. Others who are better equipped have higher qualifications and families providing them with a safety net. These fortunate youngsters can make use of the new opportunities and lead their lives in accordance with their individual wishes (Furlong & Cartmel, 1997; du Bois-Reymond, 1998).

From a *gender* perspective, it is no longer possible to classify young women as disadvantaged. A look at their educational accomplishments shows that those who underachieve are male students rather than their female peers. However, with regard to unemployment, southern Europe shows dramatic levels of female youth unemployment whereas this is the case for more young men in the north (and east) of Europe. Young women all across Europe face structural conditions that are detrimental to their wishes and needs: inhibited career opportunities in terms of pay gaps and glass ceilings, combined with a lack of public child care (European Commission, 2005). With regard to *ethnicity*, old and new inequalities accumulate in almost all European countries. School failure, discriminatory practices in education and on the labor market, and subcultural lifestyles and coping strategies interact, triggering mechanisms of marginalization (López Blasco, McNeish, & Walther, 2003).

Although inequality primarily meant different social status and different prospects of social mobility in the Fordist period, the focus shifts toward emerging risks of social exclusion in post-Fordist times (Castel, 2002). Inequality now forces young people into a race from the "wild zones" of risky transitions toward the "tame zones" of stable careers (Kelly, 1999).

Inequality is reproduced by individual decision making, which is shaped by differently socialized aspirations and different resources and opportunities to realize them individually. Where modernization processes weaken collective patterns and institutional trajectories, individual motivation—that is, the relation between subjective interest and a subjective feeling of self-efficacy—becomes a crucial factor of social integration (Bandura, 1997). It relates to both opportunities and resources. The dialectic between structure and agency is reflected in decisions on such issues as continuing one's education versus leaving school with low qualifications; the preparedness to wait for the right job to come versus withdrawing from the formal transition system and preferring a status zero, or having children versus postponing family formation to a later stage of one's life.

Given the duality of structure and agency, social reproduction primarily manifests itself as a tension between systemic restrictions and subjective needs. Whereas the systemic perspective relates to such objectively measurable career factors as qualifications or employment, the subjective perspective of individuals may be paraphrased by satisfaction and well-being (Antonovsky, 1987; Keupp et al., 1999; Walther et al., 2002). In short, destandardization means that youth transitions no longer follow institutionalized trajectories but have become individual mixtures of socioeconomic and institutional structures and subjective motivation and agency.

Diversification of Transition Patterns Between School and Work

To what extent is the destandardization of youth transitions confirmed by empirical evidence? Evans and Heinz (1994; see also Evans, Behrens, & Kaluza, 2000) introduce the concept of transition patterns to analyze how structure and agency are related in individual transitions and how these transitions relate to institutionally prescribed trajectories. Although a representative analysis of these issues would require large-scale studies combining quantitative and qualitative approaches, the available evidence is more explorative in nature and biased toward problematic transitions. This also

NEW DIRECTIONS FOR CHILD AND ADOLESCENT DEVELOPMENT • DOI: 10.1002/cad

holds true for the YOYO project, in the course of which young people were asked to narrate their transitions. Based on these interviews, the researchers identified the different phases they had gone through and developed charts for the complexity, length, and direction of the transition processes. The labels smooth, alternative, repaired, stagnant, and downward are slightly modified versions of the categories developed by Evans and Heinz. They denote different forms of the interplay between structure and agency in relation to the institutional assumptions of a linear life course. However, we must keep in mind that these patterns are formed at a certain point in time and are related to age. Hence, they do not necessarily indicate the youngsters' further life-course development. In the future, young persons may well shift from one category to another. We need to consider these developments when interpreting results. In the following sections, we discuss various transition patterns, taking into account such variables as age, education, gender, and socioeconomic background. The statements of the young people are taken from the YOYO research project (Walther et al., 2006).

Smooth Transitions. Despite a general trend of destandardization, a large share of young people follow a more or less continuous, institutionally predictable transition from education to employment. Those with a smooth transition to employment get a stable job as soon as they obtain their educational qualification. They typically do not fail at school and do not switch between temporary (precarious) jobs and unemployment spells. Young people with smooth transition patterns either get sufficient support by their teachers and parents or do not need assistance. When they complete school, they have a fairly clear idea what they want to study or do as work. Smooth transition patterns clearly depend on the ability of local labor markets to absorb school leavers as well as on the degree to which education and vocational training tally with available jobs. Gender preferences in the choices are decisive for the different unemployment rates of young men and women. As a rule, young men tend to go for vocational routes whereas young women are overrepresented in educational settings. Smooth transitions correspond to normal life plans of young people. However, there are huge differences as regards motivational investment. One might assume that following prescribed routes requires a low level of individual decision making. However, for many young people, this proves to be an exacting task that they cannot master without continually motivating themselves. One example is Leslie-Anne, 18, from Northern Ireland. Despite school problems that forced her to repeat a class, she obtained the qualification that enabled her to pursue her occupational aspirations:

> I didn't like most subjects . . . in the first to second years I was in special needs class for English. . . . Childcare was all I really wanted to do, so I didn't really care about the rest of the things.

Institutionally Repaired Transitions. Because of destandardization, the transitions of a growing number of young people are interrupted—for example, by early school leaving, unemployment, or family crises. This entails a greater need for assistance by specialized agencies that offer counseling and reorientation, retraining, further training, or reintegration into the labor market to "repair" impaired transitions. Young people in this category tend to be older than their peers with comparable trajectories. The number of repaired transitions depends on the extent to which transitions are affected by youth unemployment or unreliable links of mainstream education or training. Possibilities to reenter the mainstream system or a parallel system of compensatory remedial measures, or both, are also important. Young people with low qualifications, and in particular young men, prevail in this group whereas segmented labor market entry tends to force more young women to try something else. Access to compensatory measures can also differ for the two genders. In this connection, individual agency and motivation play a key role. Support may influence the motivational careers of young people, but they also have to be motivated to search for and accept support. One example is Orkan, aged 23, a young German with an immigration background. After a series of school failures and criminal offences, he was aided by youth workers in getting an apprenticeship, which he accepted only to improve his chances at a pending trial:

> I said to myself, I will continue until the trial, then I leave. . . . But the longer I was there, the more my interest grew—to get a good qualification, to be really involved.

Alternative Transitions. The transition process of the young people in this category does not follow predictable patterns. They may get an education exceeding normal standards, or they may leave the institutionalized pathway and opt for one that offers them personal satisfaction rather than social or economic success and security. They may, for example, go for self-employment, which entails risks while providing personal fulfillment. In their transitions, these young people experience more interruptions and zigzag movements than their peers in other transition categories, but they are determined to accomplish their often-self-defined goals. Because middle or higher socioeconomic backgrounds prevail in this category, we conclude that family support and cultural capital are also important factors for such transitions. In a number of cases, the young people's success was facilitated by transition agencies that did more than just help them pursue a regular path by encouraging and backing their unconventional decisions and goals. Gender differences are minimal in this group. Because alternative transitions take time to develop, the young people in this category tend to be older than their peers in other categories. Differences across countries depend on the extent to which education systems permit the accumulation of qualifications, on the regulations of labor markets with regard to self-employment, and on the extent to which youth services force young people to adapt to standard trajectories or permit individual choices. The young people's transition biographies typically display "trendsetting" dynamics as they make their ways through or around the system, using what they need to realize their dreams or plans by combining formal and informal ways of learning and support (see Diepstraten, du Bois-Reymond, & Vinken, 2006; Chapter Four in this volume). Others do not set out with a grand plan but manage or balance their transition successfully in the face of such structural adversities as blocked labor market entry, low educational credentials, or disadvantaged social or economic backgrounds (or both). Alternative transitions require a high level of intrinsic motivation to leave predefined pathways and to constantly reflect on and invest in one's own transition. Celia, 21, from Portugal describes her decision to become a dancer:

> Before, I wasn't sure what to do. I would always try the easiest way. . . . But then, I realized, vocation is something real. I found out I live for dance. . . . To be a dancer, a person must love it, because it's something that comes from inside.

Stagnant Transitions. As the mismatch between education and employment grows, an increasing share of young people is stuck in a vicious cycle in which temporary or precarious jobs alternate with unemployment, educational dropout, and participation in recurrent training or placement schemes. This prevents them from getting closer to an adult status that is based on stable employment. Young people in this category frequently have a poor socioeconomic background, which is documented by their problematic school careers. Moreover, their lacking biographical progress is also linked with high youth unemployment and a mismatch between education and labor market demands. Apparently the programs targeted at these youngsters were able neither to change their unfavorable situations nor to increase their motivation. Structural and individual aspects often reinforce each other. Many young people simply do not know which pathway they want to pursue or become demotivated in the course of their educational and occupational careers. By definition, stagnation refers to a longer transition period without progress and does not apply to those in the early stage of their transition. Although some young people show considerable motivation even after a series of failures, their plans are mostly short-lived, and they tend to passively wait for something to happen. Lars, 20, from Denmark explains:

> My problem is that I can't motivate myself to take an education if I do not know what I want. It's hard to find a way if you do not know the goal.

Downward Transitions. This category comprises only a small number of young people. Downward transitions can often be attributed to such difficult life events as family problems, dropping out of school, drug use, long spells of unemployment, legal prosecution, or other critical incidents and have their roots in the youngsters' poor socioeconomic backgrounds.

Young people in this category run a high risk of social marginalization or have already been marginalized and tend to live in deprived urban areas. In the YOYO study, men were slightly overrepresented as compared with women, a finding that is confirmed by other studies (MacDonald & Marsh, 2005). The more negative experiences such young people have, the more they are inclined to leave conventional pathways because they lack subjectively meaningful goals and access to recognized resources and strategies. Marginalization is often reinforced by strategies embedded in subcultures that protect fragile identities. One example is 19-year-old Özkan of Germany but of Turkish origin who struggles with restricted choices and experiences of ethnic discrimination:

> The boss said, "I'll have a cup of coffee, and you carry up the tiles"—to the sixth floor. I asked, "OK, since when do we have slavery again?" He said, "If you don't like it, just leave." And I didn't like it, so I left.

Transition Regimes Across Europe: Trends and Differences

The destandardization and, in particular, the growing insecurity associated with young people's transitions constitute a tremendous challenge for the institutions committed to regulating the life course. As a consequence, a number of policy sectors primarily attempt to repair transitions exposed to risks and ruptures. Youth policy, education and training, welfare, and labor market policies are the key sectors. Depending on their priorities and their power to structure young men's and women's lives, they can be classified as either "soft" or "hard." Economic policies, health, housing, transportation, and law are also important players in this game (Walther et al., 2006).

Youth policy belongs to the soft category because it aims at enabling young people to experiment, to actively participate in society, and to learn in nonformal settings in their leisure time. Activities are mostly organized at the local level with limited competencies and funds. Education or training and welfare are in an intermediate position. On the one hand, they deal with individual development and social rights; on the other hand, it is their task to reproduce the labor force. In doing so, they are increasingly requested to keep public expenditures for social costs low. Both sectors have larger budgets than youth policy and try to find a balance between national policy frameworks and local delivery. Finally, labor market policies address youth transitions in terms of increasing young people's employability and mediating between labor supply and demand. Hard policy sectors are directly related to school-to-work transitions; soft policies are preventive and approach young people in a more holistic way.

Although soft policies usually target all young people and hard policies rely on selective mechanisms, policies focusing on problems in transitions from school to work selectively refer to disadvantaged youth. Across policy measures and countries, we can identify two types of defining and addressing disadvantage:

> In a diagnosis focusing on structures, young people are considered disadvantaged when they are unemployed. Countries adhering to this view, among them many with high youth unemployment, have sought to solve the problem by introducing structure-related policies to increase the demand for labor.

The view that young people are unemployed because they are disadvantaged is based on the idea of individual skills deficits, lacking work ethics, or both. Countries subscribing to this viewpoint tend to have lower youth unemployment rates and to devise policies that aim at increasing young people's employability (see following definition). This approach is increasingly being mainstreamed by European Union policies.

We may, therefore, conclude that "disadvantage" is a social construction, which depends on socioeconomic, institutional, and historical contexts because it is based on the assumption that standard careers and full employment are still possible. Defining disadvantage is further complicated by such structural and individual aspects as labor market segmentation and subjective motivation. A structure-related concept may be more pertinent because it does not individualize problems caused by socioeconomic restructuring. In contrast, policies that individualize disadvantage have to be rated as mechanisms legitimizing unequal life chances caused by the discrepancy between an individual's aspirations and competitiveness. In general, it seems more appropriate to refer to *constellations of disadvantage* than to focus on individual or group characteristics (Goffman, 1962; Walther et al., 2006).

Global competition increases the pressure on national welfare states. This also affects both soft and hard youth policies and especially those focusing on disadvantaged youth. Ever since the 1990s, such concepts as employability, lifelong learning, activation, and citizenship have been mainstreamed through the European integration process:

- *Employability,* a term developed in the United Kingdom under Margaret Thatcher's rule, has become the main reference for developing active labor market policies. It is based on an individualized understanding of disadvantage according to which most unemployed are insufficiently adapted to the demands of potential employers, be it in skills or wage aspirations (European Commission, 2005).
- *Lifelong learning* reflects the fact that education and employment are no longer directly linked in post-Fordist labor markets. This has rendered time-limited preparatory school and training phases outdated and forced people to continually update their skills. Moreover, this concept integrates formal, nonformal, and informal learning into all areas of life, though it remains unclear how informal skills and knowledge can be validated to secure their integrative potential (European Commission, 2001a).

- *Activation* is closely related, with the shift toward active labor market policies aiming at employability and lifelong learning. In both cases, the state increasingly expects individuals to actively contribute to their inclusion process. Although employability ironically implies that an active individual is responsible for being (passively) employed by someone else, lifelong learning shifts the responsibility from the state to the individual. Occupational aspirations can no longer be justified by invoking educational credentials awarded by the public education system. Activation policies rely on motivating individuals to look for a job. However, the extent to which such approaches are based on the carrots-and-sticks principle ranges from models securing a decent livelihood in the Nordic countries to repressive workfare systems in the United Kingdom (Lødemel & Trickey, 2001; van Berkel & Hornemann Møller, 2002; Walther et al., 2006).

- *Citizenship* apparently has little in common with labor market integration but refers to the discourse around the civil society and (soft) youth policies (European Commission, 2001b). Reference is being made to voluntary engagement in nongovernmental organizations of the third sector, to social capital building, and to young people's active participation in youth councils. However, the fact that this discourse breaks with the trinity of civil, political, and social rights by which Marshall (1950) conceptualized citizenship in the 1950s is frequently forgotten. The simultaneity of the civil society discourse and activation policies suggests that citizenship is disconnected from the welfare state and restricted to soft policy sectors.

Their reference to individuals as coproducers of welfare definitely makes current discourses ambiguous. In this sense, they may be interpreted as taking into account the interaction between structure and agency, recognizing individual rights in a normative democratic perspective. However, this trend can also be interpreted in terms of *individualizing governance*. From this viewpoint, citizens are increasingly held responsible for their life chances and their own social integration, which is legitimized by a normative reference to individuals' subjectivities (Foucault, 1994; Rose, 1999).

So far, we have discussed transitions and policies in general. However, European diversity requires a differentiated approach. For an overview and a better understanding of key differences, we have divided the countries into clusters of *transition regimes*. The notion of "regimes" implies that "normality" is contingent not only on the very structure of transition systems but also on their relation with education, the labor market, or the welfare state and underlying cultural assumptions. Society and individuals infer from this normality what "youth transitions" are about and which collective demands and individual aspirations are legitimate. A typology of transition regimes can build on existing comparisons of welfare regimes (Esping-Andersen, 1990; Gallie & Paugam, 2000). However, these regimes also comprise labor market structures, policies to fight youth unemployment and concepts of disadvantage, mechanisms of doing gender, and different notions of youth in the sense of dominant expectations of young people (Walther, 2006). We can distinguish the following regimes:

- The *universalistic* transition regime is typical for Nordic countries (for example, Denmark), where universal welfare rights are linked to young people's citizenship status. This regime offers comprehensive schooling, a flexible training system, broad access to higher education and the labor market thanks to a large public sector, and a high degree of gender equality. Extensive counseling facilitates young people's personal development, which may also proceed along alternative pathways.
- The *liberal* transition regime is typically found in such Anglo-Saxon countries as Ireland and the United Kingdom. Its characteristics are diversity of access due to flexible education, training, and labor markets and a focus on individual responsibility through workfare with increasing risks and inequality. The liberal notion is limited to the overall aim of making young people economically independent as soon as possible while state intervention has increased, especially in education.
- Typical features of the *employment-centered* transition regime in such continental countries as Germany and the Netherlands are selective schooling and standardized training to secure a core segment of smooth transitions. This regime offers only few alternatives for entering the world of work. Prevocational routes for disadvantaged youth who wish to repair their transitions tend to be stigmatized, and social assistance is not granted on a universal level. All this reinforces stagnant transition patterns.
- The *subprotective* transition regime (found in Italy, Portugal, or Spain) offers comprehensive schooling but lacks training routes and access to benefits. Fragmented active labor market policies, long dependency on families of origin, informal work, and precarious jobs play an important role. Trajectories are strongly gendered; young people lack a clear social status. Hence, most transitions show a stagnant pattern over long periods of time.
- The transition regime(s) of *postsocialist* countries in central and eastern Europe (for example, in Romania) require further comparative analysis before they can be classified. These countries share a past in which trajectories were rigidly steered but reliable. Since the 1990s, most of them have tried to adapt their systems to the liberal or the employment-centered model with built-in subprotective structures. The result is a large number of alternative and stagnant transitions patterns.

Whereas the individualizing policy discourse mentioned above serves as a framework of reference for all these contexts, it is evident that meanings and consequences vary. Somewhat simplifying matters, we may say that self-responsibility is backed by individual social rights in the universalistic regime, but it is imposed more coercively in liberal regimes. In the employment-centered regime, this increasingly holds true for those who do not profit from the security provisions granted with standard employment whereas the deficit in terms of Fordist welfare structures also affects the shift toward activation in the subprotective regime. In postsocialist transformation countries, different and sometimes contradicting developments occur simultaneously, and individualization proceeds at a much faster pace than in the rest of Europe.

Conclusions

It is obvious that transition policies not only react but also contribute to the destandardization of youth transitions. Policy measures can support young men and women in insecure transitions, but they also involve new demands and risks. Especially if the yardstick is a standard life course that no longer matches socioeconomic realities and sociocultural normalities, such measures tend to produce "misleading trajectories" (Walther et al., 2002). It may be argued that the latter are reproduced by transition research, which has adopted the institutional view that transitions from youth to adulthood are nothing but school-to-work transitions and a dichotomy of success versus failure. Empirical evidence for the growing diversity of transition patterns suggests that policies aimed at compensating disadvantage tend to mask both persisting inequalities and the structural possibilities of full employment. This is especially the case in the employment-centered transition regime where support is most closely linked to standard trajectories whereas rough transitions tend to be addressed exclusively in terms of deviation and deficit. In contrast, the scope for biographical construction is widest in the universalistic transition regime, where social rights are linked to citizenship status.

The analysis of transition patterns also reveals the close relation between structure and agency in contributing to young people's disadvantage in school-to-work transitions. Restricted choices and opportunities undermine subjective motivation while coping strategies adopted because of lacking access to recognized resources are likely to increase marginalization. Hence, there is a need for more emphasis on the analysis of successful transitions and alternative biographies to determine the prerequisites for coping mechanisms and resilience under conditions of uncertainty and risk. To what extent can self-determined alternative transitions serve as models for transition policies targeting disadvantaged groups of youth? How can they provide room for intrinsic motivation? Choice, experiments, and trust seem to be core prerequisites. The lesson to learn for both policy and research may be that they should stop addressing youth transitions solely in terms of success or failure and approach them from the viewpoint of citizenship and active participation.

Note

1. YOYO is the acronym for Youth Policy and Participation: Potentials of Participation and Informal Learning in Young People's Transitions to the Labor Market. The project was funded by the European Commission between 2001 and 2004. Under the coordina-

tion of the Institute of Regional Innovation and Social Research (IRIS) in Tübingen, Germany, research teams from Copenhagen (Denmark), Dresden and Munich (Germany), Cork (Ireland), Bologna (Italy), Leiden (Netherlands), Lisbon (Portugal), Bucharest (Romania), Valencia (Spain), and Coleraine (Ulster, UK) were involved. More information can be obtained from the project's Web site: http://www.iris-egris.de/yoyo and Walther, du Bois-Reymond, & Biggart, 2006.

References

Alheit, P., & Dausien, B. (2000). "Biographicity" as a basic resource of lifelong learning. In P. Alheit, J. Beck, E. Kammler, R. Taylor, and H. Salling Olesen (Eds.), *Lifelong learning inside and outside of schools* (pp. 400–422). Roskilde, Denmark: Roskilde University.

Antonovsky, A. (1987). *Unraveling the mystery of health: How people manage stress and stay well.* San Francisco: Jossey-Bass.

Bandura, A. (1997). *Self-efficacy: The exercise of control.* New York: Freeman.

Castel, R. (2002). *From manual workers to wage laborers: Transformation of the social question.* New Brunswick, NJ: Transaction.

Diepstraten, I., du Bois-Reymond, M., & Vinken, H. (2006). Trendsetting learning biographies: Concepts of navigating through late modern life and learning. *Journal of Youth Studies, 9*(2), 175-193.

du Bois-Reymond, M. (1998). "I don't want to commit myself yet": Young people's life-concepts. *Journal of Youth Studies, 1*(1), 63–79.

Esping-Andersen, G. (1990). *The three worlds of welfare capitalism.* Cambridge, U.K.: Cambridge University Press.

European Commission (2001a). *Making a European area of lifelong learning a reality.* Luxemburg: Office for Official Publications of the European Communities.

European Commission (2001b). *A new impetus for European youth: A Commission white paper.* Luxemburg: Office for Official Publications of the European Communities.

European Commission (2005). *Indicators for monitoring the 2005 employment guidelines.* Luxemburg: Office for Official Publications of the European Communities.

European Group for Integrated Social Research (EGRIS). (2001). Misleading trajectories: Transition dilemmas of young adults in Europe. *Journal of Youth Studies, 4*(1), 101–119.

Evans, K., Behrens, M., & Kaluza, J. (2000). *Learning and work in the risk society: Lessons for the labor market of Europe from eastern Germany.* Houndsmill Basingstoke, U.K.: Macmillan.

Evans, K., & Heinz, W. R. (Eds.) (1994). *Becoming adults in England and Germany.* London: Anglo-German Foundation.

Foucault, M. (1994). La gouvernementalité. In *Dits et Ecrits III* (pp. 635–657). Paris: Edition Gallimard.

Furlong, A., & Cartmel, F. (1997). *Young people and social change: Individualization and risk in late modernity.* Buckingham, U.K.: Open Press.

Gallie, D., & Paugam, S. (2000). *Welfare regimes and the experience of unemployment in Europe.* Oxford, U.K.: Oxford University Press.

Giddens, A. (1984). *The constitution of society.* Cambridge, U.K.: Polity Press.

Goffman, E. (1962). On "cooling the mark out": Some aspects of adaptation and failure. In A. Rose (Ed.), *Human behavior and social processes* (pp. 482–505). Boston: Houghton.

Kelly, P. (1999). Wild and tame zones: Regulating the transitions of youth at risk. *Journal of Youth Studies, 2*(2), 193–213.

Keupp, H., Ahbe, T., Gmür, W., Höfer, R., Kraus, W., Mitzscherlich, B., & Straus, F. (1999). *Identitätskonstruktionen: Das Patchwork der Identitäten in der Spätmoderne* [Identity constructions: The patchwork of identities in late modernity]. Reinbek, Germany: Rowohlt.

Kohli, M. (1985). Die Institutionalisierung des Lebenslaufs: Historische Befunde und theoretische Argumente [The institutionalization of the life course]. *Kölner Zeitschrift für Soziologie und Sozialpsychologie, 37*(1), 1–29.

Lødemel, I., & Trickey, H. (2001). *An offer you can't refuse: Workfare in an international perspective.* Bristol: Policy Press.

López Blasco, A., McNeish, W., & Walther, A. (Eds.) (2003). *Young people and contradictions of inclusion: Towards integrated transition policies in Europe.* Bristol: Policy Press.

MacDonald, R., & Marsh, J. (2005). *Disconnected youth: Growing up in Britain's poor neighbourhoods.* Basingstoke, U.K.: Palgrave Macmillan.

Marshall, T. H. (1950). *Class, citizenship, and social development.* Chicago: University of Chicago Press.

Müller, W., & Gangl, M. (Eds.) (2003). *Transitions from education to work in Europe: The integration of youth into EU labor markets.* Oxford, U.K.: Oxford University Press.

Musgrove, F. (1964). *Youth and social order.* London: Routledge.

Myles, J. (1991). Is there a post-Fordist life course? In W. R. Heinz (Ed.), *Theoretical advances in life course research* (pp. 171–185). Weinheim, Germany: Deutscher Studienverlag.

Pais, J. M. (2000). Transitions and youth cultures: Forms and performances. *International Social Science Journal/UNESCO, 164,* 219–232.

Plug, W., Zeijl, E., & du Bois-Reymond, M. (2003). Young people's perceptions on youth and adulthood. *Journal of Youth Studies, 6*(2), 127–144.

Rose, N. (1999). *The powers of freedom: Reframing political thought.* Cambridge, U.K.: Cambridge University Press.

van Berkel, R., & Hornemann Møller, I. (Eds.) (2002). *Active social policies in the EU: Integration through participation?* Bristol: Policy Press.

Walther, A. (2006). Regimes of youth transitions: Choice, flexibility, and security in young people's experiences across different European contexts. *Young, 14*(2), 119-139.

Walther, A., du Bois-Reymond, M., & Biggart, A. (Eds.) (2006). *Participation in transition?* Frankfurt am Main: Lang.

Walther, A., Stauber, B., Biggart, A., du Bois-Reymond, M., Furlong, A., López Blasco, A., Mørch, S., & Pais, J. M. (Eds.) (2002). *Misleading trajectories: Integration policies for young adults in Europe?* Opladen, Germany: Leske/Budrich.

Williamson, H. (1997). Status zero youth and the "underclass": Some considerations. In R. MacDonald (Ed.), *Youth, the "underclass" and social exclusion* (pp. 70–82). London: Routledge.

ANDREAS WALTHER is senior researcher at the Institute for Regional Innovation and Social Research (IRIS) in Tübingen, Germany. He also teaches social pedagogy in the Department of Education at the University of Tübingen. His research focuses on youth transitions in an international perspective.

WIM PLUG worked as a sociological researcher at the University of Leiden, the Netherlands. His research focused on young people's life courses, their transition from education to work, their labor market attitudes, and their transition to adulthood in both national and European perspectives.

NEW DIRECTIONS FOR CHILD AND ADOLESCENT DEVELOPMENT • DOI: 10.1002/cad

INDEX

Back Issue/Subscription Order Form

Copy or detach and send to:

Jossey-Bass, A Wiley Imprint, 989 Market Street, San Francisco CA 94103-1741
Call or fax toll-free: Phone 888-378-2537 6:30AM–3PM PST; Fax 888-481-2665

Back Issues: Please send me the following issues at $29 each
(Important: please indicate the New Directions title initials and issue
numbers—for example, "CD99" for New Directions in Child and Adolescent
Development, number 99.)

_____

_____

_____

$ _____ Total for single issues

$ _____ SHIPPING CHARGES: SURFACE   Domestic   Canadian
                              First Item $5.00 $6.00
                              Each Add'l Item $3.00 $1.50

For next-day and second-day delivery rates, call the number listed above.

Subscriptions   Please ___ start ___ renew my subscription to *New Directions*
                for Child and Adolescent Development for the year 2_____ at the
                following rate:

                U.S.   ___ Individual $90   ___ Institutional $240
                Canada   ___ Individual $90   ___ Institutional $280
                All Others   ___ Individual $114   ___ Institutional $314

Online subscriptions are available via Wiley InterScience!

For more information about online subscriptions visit
www.wileyinterscience.com

$_____ Total single issues and subscriptions (Add appropriate sales tax for
your state for single issue orders. No sales tax for U.S. subscriptions.
Canadian residents, add GST for subscriptions and single issues.)

___ Payment enclosed (U.S. check or money order only)
___ VISA ___ MC ___ AmEx # _____ Exp. Date _____

Signature _____ Day Phone _____
___ Bill Me (U.S. institutional orders only. Purchase order required.)

Purchase order # _____
                    Federal Tax ID13559302   **GST 89102 8052**

Name _____

Address _____

_____

Phone _____ E-mail _____

For more information about Jossey-Bass, visit our Web site at www.josseybass.com

OTHER TITLES AVAILABLE IN THE
NEW DIRECTIONS FOR CHILD AND ADOLESCENT DEVELOPMENT SERIES
Reed W. Larson and Lene Arnett Jensen, Editors-in-Chief
William Damon, Founding Editor-in-Chief

NEW DIRECTIONS FOR
CHILD AND ADOLESCENT DEVELOPMENT
IS NOW AVAILABLE ONLINE AT WILEY INTERSCIENCE

What is Wiley InterScience?

Wiley InterScience is the dynamic online content service from John Wiley & Sons delivering the full text of over 300 leading scientific, technical, medical, and professional journals, plus major reference works, the acclaimed Current Protocols laboratory manuals, and even the full text of select Wiley print books online.

What are some special features of Wiley InterScience?

Wiley Interscience Alerts is a service that delivers table of contents via e-mail for any journal available on Wiley InterScience as soon as a new issue is published online.
EarlyView is Wiley's exclusive service presenting individual articles online as soon as they are ready, even before the release of the compiled print issue. These articles are complete, peer-reviewed, and citable.
CrossRef is the innovative multi-publisher reference linking system enabling readers to move seamlessly from a reference in a journal article to the cited publication, typically located on a different server and published by a different publisher.

How can I access Wiley InterScience?

Visit http://www.interscience.wiley.com.

Guest Users can browse Wiley InterScience for unrestricted access to journal tables of contents and article abstracts, or use the powerful search engine.
Registered Users are provided with a *Personal Home Page* to store and manage customized alerts, searches, and links to favorite journals and articles. Additionally, Registered Users can view free online sample issues and preview selected material from major reference works.
Licensed Customers are entitled to access full-text journal articles in PDF, with select journals also offering full-text HTML.

How do I become an Authorized User?

Authorized Users are individuals authorized by a paying Customer to have access to the journals in Wiley InterScience. For example, a university that subscribes to Wiley journals is considered to be the Customer. Faculty, staff, and students authorized by the university to have access to those journals in Wiley InterScience are Authorized Users. Users should contact their library for information on which Wiley journals they have access to in Wiley InterScience.

ASK YOUR INSTITUTION ABOUT WILEY INTERSCIENCE TODAY!